GERMAN LITERATURE OF THE NINETEENTH CENTURY

GERMAN LITERATURE
OF THE
NINETEENTH CENTURY

by Hermann Boeschenstein

Edward Arnold

© Hermann Boeschenstein, 1969
First published 1969 by
Edward Arnold (Publishers) Ltd.
41 Maddox Street, London W1

cloth edition SBN: 7131 5454 3
paper edition SBN: 7131 5455 1

Printed in Great Britain by
Billing and Sons, Limited, Guildford and London

Acknowledgement

While I must take sole responsibility for the arrangement and treatment of my material, and especially for a preference for seeing the development of literature as not so much concomitant to as interwoven with the hopes and aims of a progressive social and political evolution, I cannot be grateful enough to two of my colleagues for their many-sided support. Professor Margaret Sinden and Professor William Packer have rendered invaluable assistance in the preparation of the manuscript and the clarification of so many of my comments and evaluations. Their help has turned an at times difficult task into a stimulating and gratifying experience.

H.B.

Contents

1   *Introduction*

It is customary to speak of the nineteenth century in German literature without pedantic regard for the calendar. A few years can be lopped off at either end. 1815 is a likely start, if we take our cue from political history, but we can also wait longer, for the terminus indicated by Goethe's death in 1832, and the ebbing away of romanticism soon after. At the other end of the century one feels tempted to stop with the great representatives of realistic fiction, and to push Hauptmann, George, Hofmannsthal, Ricarda Huch and others into the new century, though their beginnings fall into the last decade of the old one. In terms of literary periods—not one of our main concerns—this would make nineteenth-century literature that of 'Biedermeier' and Young Germany, from 1815, or as others would have it, from 1830 to 1848, the years of the restoration and the Metternich regime, followed by realism, whose death-knell some naturalists began to sound in the early Nineties—though the expressionists thought differently and set the decisive caesura, the one that marks off, not one school from another, but tradition from modernity, around 1910. Judged by the criterion of ethical convictions and social thought, however, the tradition of the nineteenth century extended into the Thirties of the twentieth.

The existence of this tradition, the strengthening of its optimistic, hopeful note is, to our mind, the most impressive phenomenon in the nineteenth century. The age seemed to be imbued with the spirit of Leibniz, notwithstanding the presence and influence of Schopenhauer. On closer inspection we notice that while Friedrich Schlegel's dictum that all human activities would henceforth be directed with increasing vigour towards a millennium on earth turned out to be a most accurate prophecy, fulfilled with astonishing tenacity by many writers of the nineteenth century and beyond, there was side by side with this socio-political engagement a growing feeling of doubt and insecurity, intensified perhaps by Schopenhauer, about man's ability to conceive more than ephemeral values. While outwardly a front of persuasive progressiveness was presented, the shafts of despair drove inward, to reveal irremediable flaws in the nature of human beings. The confession of this discord between thinking and feeling, or between public admission and private reservation, occurs sometimes in the life as well as in the work of an author, sometimes only in the one. Successive collapses of the structures supposed to give support—Christian and humanistic ethics, Hegelian philosophy and scientific positivism—can be blamed for the loss of faith in a purposeful existence. Not even the appeal to man's indubitable and instinctively felt obligation to solidarity with all mankind and to his inborn socialistic nature was strong enough to stave off a sense of expendability, much as these factors have done and are still doing to hold us on the course of that optimism which by and large remains the great distinction of nineteenth-century German literature.

Another no less characteristic feature is a well-nigh irresistible trend towards realism and reality. Fritz Martini designates the period from 1848 to 1898 as that of bourgeois realism. This trend, is, of course, an integral part of the European tradition dating from the Renaissance and reinforced by English, French, and German philosophers of subsequent eras. Man's faculties are regarded as adequate for knowing the world we live in, and its many still unexplored physical and psychological regions present an enthusiastically accepted challenge to the human mind. Today, when both intelligence and intelligibility are open to serious doubt, we can understand all the better what a joy it must have been to live in a world that was susceptible of, and waiting for, further exploration. The search for reality went on in many directions, even within the literary sphere. It was not only a question of giving the aspirations and declarations of classical and romantic art a more definite place in time and geography, or of reversing the traditional process by getting hold of the concrete phenomena first and then extracting from them some general, if not universal, meaning. What was more urgent was to realize and fill the many gaps left open in the literary awareness and presentation of our fellow-men. The rural world had hardly been entered, and it was one of the glorious achievements of the early nineteenth century to discover and use peasant life for creative purposes. Industrial, or rather proletarian, environments were to follow later—but we must not forget that the middle classes themselves had been vastly ignored or, which is almost the same, distorted beyond recognition. Bourgeois realism is not solely a realistic outlook practised by bourgeois writers, but a sincerely objective attempt to understand the middle classes and to assign them their task in the re-emergence of enlightenment and humanism which the nineteenth century was.

Through the same impulse the world at large, and not only German-speaking countries, was begging to become better known. Though the complaint that travelling by train or boat does little to increase our knowledge and much to make us opinionated recurs from Immermann to Fontane, interest in foreign countries was growing and could not be ignored. North America is now discovered for the second time and either eagerly sought, as in Ernst Willkomm's novel *Die Europamüden* (1838), or found wanting and rejected, as in Ferdinand Kürnberger's *Der Amerika-Müde* (1855). But this was, of course, not to prevent further journeys, by steam or imagination, across the seven seas. There were other ways of learning to know the outside world. The enthusiastic acceptance of Scott and even more so of Dickens in German translations is a matter of record. Balzac, Tolstoy, Dostoevski, and Ibsen had, if anything, an influence of even greater spread.

We need not elaborate on the relationship between science and literature in the nineteenth century. The two often worked the same veins, and for psychology and sociology literature has done valuable spade-work. Here again we are dealing with a European trend; as early as 1883 Francesco de Sanctis published his *Il darwinismo nella vita e nell' arte*, and in 1887 there appeared Wilhelm Bölsche's *Die naturwissenschaftlichen Grundlagen der Poesie*. For the realists of the nineteenth century the world was no longer the romantic creation of man, but something mysteriously present and open for inspection.

Brecht has properly pointed out that the concept of realism is marked by its breadth, not by narrowness. And this was said in connection with Shelley, whom he claims for the realists. For realistic literature does not exclude imagination or artistic values. It is no paradox to claim that Brecht widens the meaning of realism by restricting it to social realism. The latter for him is the application of a social attitude to all our activities, scientific or artistic.

Man's nature urges him to secure justice, peace and prosperity for all people—the millennium Friedrich Schlegel foresaw. And the world meets man more than half-way; realism, as Brecht remarked, is on our side, and so we have every reason to be on its side. The eager burrowing of the nineteenth century into reality is prompted by and obeys an inveterate desire to build a better world to live in.

The energetic stirring of the humane tradition which we regard as the hallmark of nineteenth-century literature, is closely allied with its realistic bent, if the two are not simply different aspects of one and the same process—a process which is basically social. The realistic view of humanity explains in part the doubt and misgivings, the despair and nihilism which, as we pointed out, cast an early shadow across the path of optimistic humanism, as an unavoidable corollary of the whole development. A realistic study of life was bound to bring its seamy sight to light. Man is in the grip of selfish instincts; even with the best of intentions we often miss the true aspects of existence and project social visions that we have to discard later. Reality has wide dimensions and is manifold and complex, to quote Brecht again. Awareness of our moral defects comes as a result of a clear-eyed look into reality, and the fright it causes us we must transform into a redoubled effort to defend our humane position. The nineteenth century does not suffer from double vision, it sees life as it is and knows that it ought to be different. Nineteenth-century literature must not be analysed as a period revealing the first symptoms of a schizophrenic mind, but studied for the resourcefulness with which it dissociated itself from corroding thought, and admired for its will to maintain a humane mood.

A deeply ingrained tradition which for the implementation of its ethical tenets required a better appraisal of reality—this sounds simple enough as a mandate for literature. But the attempted execution took place amidst complex ideas and emotions, visions and projections. One has but to remember the philosophical systems and literary trends acting and reacting on each other at the end of the eighteenth century, the explosive forces released by the romantic writers and thinkers, and the natural sciences struggling to free themselves from the cocoons of metaphysical credos, to gauge the variety of possible sorties into reality. Would the poets and writers not have been better off by taking their hints from Goethe's 'Ich singe wie der Vogel singt'? Instead, they all seem to enrol in courses on philosophy. By a neat symptomatic or symbolic arrangement fate decreed that even Gottfried Keller was to sit at the feet of Feuerbach, if not to procure the philosophical prerequisites for a poet, then at least to see his own homespun 'Weltanschauung' stamped with the specialist's approval. Grillparzer and Hebbel had submitted to a far more rigorous philosophical training and felt for ever obliged to justify the existence of the poet in a world that was used to looking to the philosopher for insight and guidance. Small wonder that German literary history, once it was prised loose from a naïve compilation of facts, insisted that its task was to treat literature within the context of 'Geistesgeschichte', reading literary texts as applications or expositions of easily identifiable philosophical systems. There is hardly any major figure in nineteenth-century writing who did not venture into philosophical or aesthetic theory, and if the writers managed to keep the spectre of 'graue Theorie' out of their fiction and poetry or drama, the backdoor of their correspondence is quite often kept wide open for it.

Such intellectual curiosity was not without danger to the creative mind, but it gave the age a deeply serious and thoughtful character. Though a number of bold thrusts and radical turns were made, in matters of form and content, a feeling that tradition had evolved a set of timeless values, the loss of which, if they were left unattended, might imperil the course of civilization, is never wholly absent and more often than not lies heavily on man's conscience. Call this a handicap to an unimpeded sprightly flow of imagination, yet such 'Pietät', in addition to reminding us of the continuity and solidarity of human efforts, bids us not to over-estimate originality and serves as a memorandum to the effect that, while such abiding ideas and emotions are in constant need of fresh, invigorating expression, our first task is to bring them to bear on the conduct of our private and communal affairs. It is when reverence for the aesthetic canons of the past becomes equal to or greater than the regard for contemporary needs that the nineteenth century assumes a stale and faded look. It must not be forgotten, however, that the unsubstantiality of preponderantly aesthetic literature is matched by the tastelessness of purely ideological writing. The true artist overcomes both dangers by the magic of the immediacy with which he touches reality. The relatedness of all phenomena with one another, the solidarity among all living beings will be heightened, in a genuine work of art, from theoretical acceptance to throbbing participation.

A century like the nineteenth, with its underlying pattern of progress—even if it is only progress towards a more pronounced realism—tempts the historian to identify advance in time with advance in artistic performance. But it is not novelty in style or content which determines the intrinsic value of a work of art. This is done by the degree of excellence in craftsmanship. The appeal of art to our aesthetic sensibilities is as much part of its *raison d'être* and functions as its ethos. A story by Stifter or Keller, a Fontane novel or a work of Raabe, though the message may now seem remote from our concerns, can give us incomparably more joy than some poorly manufactured *pièce de thèse*, no matter how deeply we feel affected by its content. There is much to be said for moving from one artistic delight to the other and forgetting all the vexing problems of historical context and sequence. German literary historians are not normally in the habit of dwelling on stylistic and formal elements, and have to be exhorted from time to time to surrender more readily to the fascination of a striking image, a perfectly wrought phrase, a skilfully joined interplay of motifs or any such *valeurs* as only *il miglior fabbro* can produce. German literature of the nineteenth century is rich in such surprises and does not have to fear comparison with any other period, as far as the sheer pleasure of felicitous expression and composition is concerned. We shall not look askance at such qualities, fearing as some ideologists do that they distract us from scrutinizing content. Aesthetic excellence, by resensitizing us to the immediacy of human experience, imparts vitality to thought and emotion and puts us on the springboard of action. And if great art seems on occasion to detach us from problematic thought, it will never fail to make us more alive to the beauty, mystery, and challenge of the human situation. Art, in order to fulfil its function in civilization, is strongly pledged to inherent aesthetic standards. Hence its double role in the history of nineteenth-century literature as in any other age: to receive, examine, refine and transmit the impulses of valuable tradition, to continue on the march to the millennium and at the same time to remind us in manifestations of arresting beauty that life can reach a maximum of satisfaction at any given time, without having to wait for the realization of our collective hopes or dreams.

One last introductory remark, not unrelated to some of the strokes we have sketched in, must be made. Even by singling out what by a wide consensus can be regarded as the important literary figures, we find that these were also the popular writers of their time. A few exceptions notwithstanding, German literature between classicism and expressionism appealed to a large audience and was within the reach of the common reader. This expansion— a democratic feature of some kind—resulted not from lowering the standards of form and content, though this was tried too, but from the ability to raise the interest of the readers in the problems of life, their own problems, and in the artistic presentation and filtration of these concerns.

2   *Epigones?*

The sixty years from the beginning of Storm and Stress to the death of Goethe showered Germany with an unheard-of wealth of artistic achievement and inspiration, of philosophical thought, scholarship, and science. Goethe's life and work alone would have sufficed to leave a heritage the like of which is seldom bequeathed to mankind. These riches, placed at the threshold of the nineteenth century, were strong determinants of what was to follow. The literary historian feels taxed to the limit by the obligation of informing himself about the Age of Goethe and is tempted to wish, for himself and for German civilization, that there had been a kind of breathing space after 1832, to sort out the past and safeguard its absorption in the years to come.

No such respite was granted. Reactions to the new situation were as different as the talents and dispositions of the younger generation. Goethe, so Thomas Mann tells us in his essay *Goethe als Repräsentant des bürgerlichen Zeitalters*, knew that his demise would release a sigh of relief: 'Ouf'! For Kleist and perhaps also for Grillparzer the event came too late; both—so it is said—felt the chilling shadow of Goethe's greatness and were unable to mature in their own ways. Be that as it may, there were others to experience and welcome a vacuum that spelt freedom from classical canons—romanticism had for the time being spent its forces—and gladly accepted the challenge of a new era. Scientists, and political and social thinkers, burning with a desire to make up for the time-lag Germany had suffered in their fields, experienced a *ver sacrum*. Why should the literary minds not do the same? They tried and soon noticed that their situation was different from that of the other intellectuals. The technologists, scientists, and sociologists had little to learn from the German past and much to gain from unprejudiced reasearch, while the poets and writers could not, in their own interest, disregard the experience of their predecessors, and spurn the advice proffered by tradition. This double obligation of marching forward and looking backward accounts for some of the characteristics of German nineteenth-century literature, at the end no less than at the beginning.

'Ouf!' Perhaps, in some quarters. A more respectable reason for enjoying freedom and at the same time feeling deeply indebted to Goethe stems from the fact that *Faust II* had been left completed. This put an end to that restless and irreverential stirring among younger writers, Grillparzer, Chamisso, Grabbe and others, to continue where Goethe after publication of *Part I* had apparently left the threads dangling. The appearance of the *Second Part* in 1833 made all this literary unrest superfluous—it is impossible to surmise how much energy the nineteenth century might otherwise have wasted on the question of what to do with Faust, after the abortive attempt to rescue Gretchen. We salute Lenau, who had the courage to give his own version of the Faust theme as late as 1839, but are happier with Friedrich Theodor Vischer's parody, *Faust: Der Tragödie dritter Teil* (1862), because it ridiculed the propensity of Germans to think that Faust is all soul, profundity and *ultima ratio*, and that all Germany resembles Faust. Goethe's *Faust* had done harm enough by putting, as the critics saw it, *Tat* at the beginning of all things, though we shall not subscribe to the view that the nineteenth century and part of the twentieth were in the clutches of an ill-advised (and un-Goethean) dynamism and that we are only now aware of the wrong path we have been led down by the idolatry of action at any price.

Karl Leberecht Immermann (1796–1840) in his novel *Die Epigonen* (1836) attempted to give a comprehensive and detailed account of the period that felt both overwhelmed and paralysed by the greatness of the past. He gives an exhaustive collection of what he considers to be symptoms of 'Epigonentum.' The time, he argues, is such that only superficial characters feel at ease, slipping merrily into the coats which the past has left us, alternately 'into the pious coat, into the historical coat, into the art coat and into God knows how many other coats'. The more serious-minded suffer for two reasons; they cannot formulate a new message and are unable to reach their contemporaries and impress them with the wisdom of the Weimar tradition. Modern forms of information and communication, a rapidly revolving kaleidoscope of impressions, fill even educated people with mere opinions on everything, without anchorage in sincere belief and sound conviction. Some of Immermann's best characters fall into a brooding that borders on nihilism. By and large, however, his bark is worse than his bite. The deadly weight of 'Epigonentum' was mostly his own personal idiosyncrasy, fostered by an apprehensive feeling that for the completion of his novel he had to lean heavily on Goethe and Jean Paul. He need not have worried unduly about that, for he took no more from them than did later novelists of repute. Certain typical constellations and archetypal characters are bound to recur in novels of panoramic dimensions. Besides, there is much that is new in *Die Epigonen*, and the very decision Hermann, the protagonist, is ultimately faced with, after protracted shadow-boxing with the past, strikes a modern chord. He finally falls heir to an aristocratic title and to an industrial establishment developed by his uncle. The former he cannot accept, after his many brushes with the nobility, and the latter he will take over only with strong reservations. 'The factories will have to be closed and the land restored to agriculture. I must regard these establishments for the satisfaction of artificial demands as downright pernicious and evil. The earth belongs to the plough, to the sun and rain which mature the seed, and to the industrious working men of simple means. Like a hurricane our time rushes towards a sterile mechanism. We cannot stop its course, but neither can we be blamed if for ourselves and our people we hedge off a small area and fortify this island as long as possible against the onrushing waves of industrial development.' Resignation or prophecy, or both? The escape into the idyllic situation is a common route in the nineteenth century. It has after the Second World War been re-evaluated, saved from the stigma of escapism and termed a farsighted directive to save mankind.

There are other aspects in *Die Epigonen* to disqualify its title. If the novel is a veritable rogues' gallery of faint-hearted characters who drift anaemically through a period that bemoans its saturation with ideas and feelings and leaves no room for originality, Immermann, by mobilizing the antidotes, creates a series of exemplary persons and situations. Discussions relate by no means to the past only but plot future courses in education and politics. The ruts of 'Epigonentum' are obviously destined to end in lethargy, but another generation, or another social class, will envisage a more hopeful future, and with a quotation from Lamartine Immermann

refutes Spengler's doctrine of the decline of the West long before
it was proclaimed. We are told that Immermann underwent a
change of heart during the French revolution of 1830, while he was
working on his novel, and that the social visions coming from
Paris made him a fellow-traveller of the Young Germans. Whether
or not he needed such help, he had his own lightning bolt with
which to bring the world of passive, timid souls crashing down. In
the novel this experience, his 'Gemütswunder', is transferred to a
medical practitioner, one of the first in a long series of doctors in
nineteenth-century literature to practise and not just to preach love
of life and love of our neighbour. The experience is that of a sudden
awareness of the existence of God, and of God in our own being.
Heart and mind fill to the brim with this certainty. God is most of
all the name for the mysterious cause of an emotion which is aglow
with the 'innocence, beauty and kindness' of the world in spite of
all its deficiencies. What is at first heat turns into a light which
reveals in detail the truth of our revelation that life is meaningful;
also, moments of such rejuvenating rapture will repeat themselves
to illumine our path through life.

In some of his minor works Immermann may show a manifest
dependence on predecessors, but in a second long narrative, *Münchhausen* (1838), he boldly strides into what was almost German *terra
incognita*, comic fiction. The work is not, as some critics claim, a
half-hearted attempt at the humorous novel, but a novel of two
easily separable parts; one of these is set up as a shooting-gallery for
the satirist, while the other provides a happy hunting-ground for
the realistic observer. Baron Münchhausen, liar and story-teller,
mountebank and swindler, has finally secured for himself a berth
in the castle of some decrepit nobleman whom he can interest in a
scheme to extract bricks from the air. Between them the two attract
all the cranks, oddities, and fantasts, timeless and of the time. As
moralist Immermann has to judge severely, but as narrator he has
his fun. The great humorous novel he may have aspired to—with
Cervantes as his lodestar—did not materialize; success came in the
other half of the book, which is often bodily lifted out of the
context and published separately as *Der Oberhof*. This is the name
of a large Westphalian farm, described with obvious relish, a
miniature world of peasant customs and mores, basically a sound

sphere and the appropriate place to give Oswald, a landed aristocrat from Southern Germany, and Lisbeth, the daughter of Münchhausen, the start for a happy and public-spirited life. While only a few hints are given as to the manner in which the young couple will represent a more hopefully active generation, the wayward composition of the novel and the open form which allows the printer and the book-binder and, of course, the author himself to appear in it, enable Immermann to digress in the direction of an essayistic novel. He envisages the coming of a third phase in European civilization, after the aesthetically sensitized ancient period and the spiritual preponder-ance of the Middle Ages. The new era will be characterized by the secularization of religion and the utilization of nature for the benefit of man. Historical religions will converge into one universal humanism, and with the mobilization of our intellectual resources fear and want will disappear. But let no one think that such progress can be made possible and permanent without the human heart leading the way. Immermann's 'Gemütswunder' has, as we said, to recur time and again, and the book ends with a well-known paean to the heart that has to serve as compass in the vessel of time, if we are to reach the shores of a better land. 'Die Weltgeschichte ist das Gewand der Gottesgeschichte'; the essence of Immermann's vision is not that of Novalis in *Die Christenheit oder Europa*, but that of Friedrich Schlegel's prophetic statement; for its fulfilment we must be ready to engage in a fearless process of secularization and to work towards the redemption of the old religious promises, peace and happiness for all on earth, by striving to harness the forces of nature inside and outside our own being.

These and other ideas bring him close to the group of writers called 'Das Junge Deutschland'. He shares with them a keen interest in politics and an ardent desire to participate in communal life, as a lawyer, civil servant, and most of all as director of the Düsseldorf Municipal Theatre, one of the leading German stages throughout the nineteenth century. Immermann saw too many tasks ahead of his generation, and took too many of them upon himself, to linger under the shadow of 'Epigonentum'. Others went through the same experience. Gutzkow, Spielhagen, and even Keller, had to overcome an initial tardiness caused by their reverence for classical standards, either by trying new forms or proclaiming fresh contents, or by both. For the dramatists Weimar was even more difficult to accept or to shake off. But the term 'epigone' as a negative epithet has now all but disappeared from histories of German literature. Pedantic imitations of classical or romantic works have been relegated to trivial literature, or they survive—mainly in the form of verse narratives—as quaint documents. Creative innovators, avant-gardists, and critics in sympathy with them, will of course continue to brand a preceding generation as 'Epigonen', but historians prefer to speak of influences whose ramifications can reappear as if from underground; they respect Spitteler's attempt to revive in his *Olympischer Frühling* (1900–05) the ancient epic as an impressive show of strength, and such authors of historical novels as Wilhelm Hauff (1802–27), Josef Victor von Scheffel (1826–86) and Robert Hamerling (1830–89), who had no German models to emulate, but went to France and England for inspiration, mainly to Walter Scott, are better called mediators than epigones. Hauff's *Lichtenstein* (1826) and Scheffel's *Ekkehard* (1855), though they have long been dropped from the list of significant fiction, stand out as favourites of unsophisticated readers and juveniles. Even the more dubious kind of historical novel as we have it in Felix Dahn's (1834–1912) *Ein Kampf um Rom* (1876) or Georg Ebers' (1837–98) *Eine ägyptische Königstochter* (1864) is not labelled 'epigonenhaft', but given the slightly more honorific term 'Professorenroman'. The writer who did the most, in the middle of the nineteenth century, to develop historical fiction was Hermann Kurz (1813–1873). Much as he profited from the study of Scott and Hauff, he brought to his craft an original and sensitive mind, and a deep affection for the common people. *Schillers Heimatjahre* (1843)—the first German novel with a prominent literary figure as its hero—and *Der Sonnenwirt* (1854) succeed both in giving a seemingly faithful picture of past events and in making these serve the concerns of a courageously progressive, democratic author.

Terms to provide for some sort of a grouping into literary periods are at best approximations. The two which provide the heading above form no exception, unless it be in the sense of an extraordinary pliability. But taken together they prove useful. They cover, at any rate from 1830 on, the same period and share the terminal year of 1848—the start of 'Biedermeier' is set at the beginning of the Metternich regime in 1815, whereas Young Germany arose with the hopes emanating from Paris in 1830. Both terms still are the subject of hotly debated argumentation, and agreement prevails on a very general basis only: 'Biedermeier' is inwardly directed, 'das Junge Deutschland' is out-going. The Metternich era elicited both these reactions, by frightening some people back into the shell of their private lives and by driving others to protest against the situation and to attempt to remedy it. Those German and foreign critics who are in the habit of dressing down German literature for its excessive cult of inwardness delve gleefully into the sentimentalism of 'Biedermeier'—they should not overlook the staunch endeavour of the Young Germans to ventilate political and social interests, even if it has to be conceded that Young Germany, unless we include Immermann, Heine and Büchner in it, has left no towering masterpieces.

'Biedermeier' writers avoid conflict with the authoritites in State and Church. They will no longer, as did the early romantics, wield their poetic gifts as a magic instrument to change reality. They restrict their concerns to the personal sphere. This inevitably led to greater attention being paid to everyday occurrences; an affectionate glance falls on things near and draws solace from the observable order or from an order which man is able to impose upon a circumscribed environment. It is not very often that this limited world falls prey to feelings of constriction or even despair. The occasional awareness of an ideal world contrasting or clashing with reality is borne with serene equanimity. M. J. Norst in J. M. Ritchie's *Periods in German Literature* says:

By the end of the first decade of this century the word 'Biedermeier' had thus come to be used for a number of concepts which can be placed roughly under three headings. It could mean: a philistine attitude and a narrow range of artistic endeavour, a lack of intellectual curiosity, a sense of uncritical acceptance, an exaggerated concern with trivialities. It could also imply: domestic tranquillity and virtue: love of 'real' things in a 'real' world because they are a pledge of eternal harmony; in fact that state of innocence in which the German and Austrian 'Bürger' was seen to live before the Fall of the Industrial Revolution—his sense of tradition, his social customs. Finally it could be used to express the idea of a period of violent political and social upheaval.

Günther Wcydt stresses the 'Biedermeier' aspects of 'Sammeln und Hegen'; he can point to a number of works in which characters are engaged in building up and attending to a collection of plants and minerals, or in gardening. Such collecting and cherishing extends to reminiscences and leaves us with the illusion that we exist in a miniature world which is as rich and interesting as its original.

Other features claimed for 'Biedermeier' are stress on moderation in content and form, a strong reliance on reason, an aversion to politics qualified by a congenital sympathy for the spirit of restoration, a preference for simple literary forms, for the genre pictures of painters such as Ludwig Richter, Moritz von Schwind and Carl Spitzweg, and a diction which mildly spices a classical vocabulary with archaic and dialect expressions.

The list of writers in which some of these so-called 'Biedermeier' attributes can be found includes Gotthelf, Raimund, Grillparzer, Stifter, Droste-Hülshoff, Mörike, Keller; needless to say, they can all be shown to have on occasion alloyed their 'Biedermeier' features with the very opposite qualities, or to be 'Biedermeier' long after the licence had expired, in 1848. Such and other terminological pins had hardly been set up before other critics came to shoot them down, and while the game may continue for some time we are prepared to take a stand even now. A more modest appraisal of the place of the artist in the world, and of the function of poetry, was a natural reaction, among some writers, to the strained demands of

classicism and more so of romanticism. Napoleon's sword proved
to be more powerful than all the pens of the German idealists, and
after Napoleon a relatively secure and tranquil existence was
eagerly yearned for; moreover, the social and political situation in
Germany and Austria after 1815 was confusing enough to allow
only two choices: either to plunge into the discussion, at the risk
of one's life, as the Young Germans did, or to withdraw and
remember Voltaire's *cultiver son jardin*. There were sufficient joys in
private life to make resignation easy and the cult of simplicity and
serenity rewarding. Anyone with a penchant for harmonizing the
welter of phenomena through self-limitation would find himself in
tune with the restoration and excused for not pursuing more ambitious schemes. The charm with which some of these allegedly
'Biedermeier' characteristics appear in the art and literature of the
period justifies the term. But with its tinge of quaintness and with-
drawal it is inapplicable to men in whom the yearning for idyllic
living became embroiled with doubt and despair, or with a vigorously stirring social conscience.

Young Germans, on the other hand, tried to make themselves
heard from a public platform. They either belonged to, or provided
the necessary ammunition for, the two opposition parties forming
around 1830, the Liberals and the Radical Democrats. They were
the non-conformists in art and literature, in social and political
philosophy, without a strong feeling of cohesion or a slogan for
their programmes until an apprehensive government provided
them with both. The 'Hambacher Fest' in 1832, two days of idle
talk by liberal spokesmen, had driven fear into the hearts of the
authorities, who now had recourse to censorship laws. The publication in 1835 of Karl Ferdinand Gutzkow's (1811–78) novel *Wally,
die Zweiflerin*, a bold discussion of political and social ideas and
amorous experiences, triggered drastic counter-measures. A decree
issued by the Frankfurt Diet in 1835 ordered all German govern-
ments to watch and if necessary to prosecute 'the writers, printers,
and distributors of works coming from the literary group known as
Young Germany'. The name had been taken from Ludolf Wienbarg's (1802–72) *Aesthetische Feldzüge* (1834), which he dedi-
cated to 'Das Junge Deutschland'. The decree unwittingly points
to the three-pronged attack of all revolutions: religious freedom,

social reforms, emancipation from sex taboos. But even if Young Germany received its intellectual impetus from the July revolution of 1830 and its historical designation from the Frankfurt Diet, there was never a strong consolidation of thought and action except that all authors stayed within a wide perimeter of liberalism, much to the annoyance of Friedrich Engels, who exempted only Börne from the accusation that they were woolly-headed phrase-makers. C. P. Magill says that 'there were in existence several Young Germanies; the men who in their own eyes were warriors in the very vanguard of human emancipation appeared to their opponents on the Right as subversive doctrinaires and to their radical critics on the Left as aimless dilettanti'.

If there was one conviction to which all Young Germans could subscribe, it was that literature should be accorded a greater share in the shaping of public life and that it must fulfil this task by an unequivocal engagement. Characteristically the aesthetic manifesto of Young Germany, Wienbarg's *Aesthetische Feldzüge*, is much stronger in proclaiming such interest in public affairs than it is in outlining experimental techniques of writing. Gutzkow, taking the pulse of the 'Zeitgeist' which literature was to serve, prescribed the formula: the aim of our period must be the citizen, no longer man as such. The stricture applies to the supposedly general and idealized features of man in his classical prototypes. That Goethe's *Wilhelm Meister* had long ago started the search for the 'Bürger'—the man who relates his ideas and activities to the community—Gutzkow had overlooked. His directives should do much to correct the widely publicized complaint that German literature of the nineteenth century was shying away from political and social interests. Young Germany, as we indicated, affected most of the writers we count among the realists, winning vociferous or tacit approval of its quest for social reforms. But what is disturbing is the slur cast by Wienbarg and others on 'delectability', the low opinion they had of this other part of the Horatian precept. Where literature is judged by its polemical verve one is likely to be satisfied with something less than artistic excellence, and many Young Germans—or all of them, according to some critics—failed to spend enough time on proper aesthetic gestation. Their contribution to the discussion of ideas proved much more influential than their poetic achievements.

E. M. Butler cuts the Gordian knot tied by the Young Germans by declaring them all to be followers of Saint-Simonism. She shows how well informed the Germans were, from 1830 on, about the social philosophy of Saint-Simon and Enfantin. Heine, in Paris since 1834, had much to do with the spreading of this social gospel, 'my new realism', as he called it. Three German women writers, Rahel Varnhagen von Ense, Bettina von Arnim and Charlotte Stieglitz, were drawn to Saint-Simon by natural affinities, embracing as they did the doctrine of harmony between the flesh and the mind. It is more difficult to claim Gutzkow, Laube, Wienbarg and others for Saint-Simonism, because there were a number of different socialistic currents running through the first half of the nineteenth century, and because political progress was fostered by a variety of liberalizing programmes. The Young Germans belong, broadly speaking, to that 'Frühsozialismus' which was later partly absorbed into Marxism, though many of their early communistic and socialistic tenets survived to compete with Marxism or to leaven it with elements of Christianity and humanism. Friedrich Schlegel's ideal of the kingdom on earth could, after all, be approached in more than one way, and not all Young Germany was in thrall to Saint-Simonism. Needless to say, neither Saint-Simonism nor any other brand of socialism carried with it a common set of stylistic practices or innovations, any more than Darwin, Schopenhauer or Nietzsche created a distinctive literary movement. Rather, they left their impact on a number of schools which in turn emphasized diverse aspects of their intellectual mentors—in the case of Nietzsche this is too obvious to need elaboration.

A more democratic social consciousness—this seems to be the common denominator of Young Germany. But other aspects have been stressed, for instance a psychological characteristic, 'Zerrissenheit', a state of being at odds with oneself. The term and the thought were borrowed from Alexander von Ungern-Sternberg's (1806–68) novel *Die Zerrissenen* (1832), in which a host of characters confess to being torn between conflicting forces, between sensuality and spirituality, a blasé existence and a devotion to high ideals, between private and political life. More often than not they nurture an inner restlessness, while in the best of cases the mood is one of helplessness among people who try in vain to translate their noble urges into useful action. Heinrich Laube (1806–84) in his novel *Das junge Europa* (1833), and Karl Gutzkow in *Blasedow und seine Söhne* (1838), best presented the picture of a period in which young men and women are moved by the spirit of liberalism to rejuvenate if not revolutionize German civilization, but find themselves thwarted both by a stifling tradition and by their own insufficiency. The authors, one must conclude, are often themselves torn between sympathetic understanding of 'Zerrissenheit' and sarcastic comments on it.

Though neither 'Biedermeier' nor Young Germany shows the compactness we associate with literary movements, it is legitimate to ask whether any great writer emerged from them, as Goethe did from Storm and Stress or Gerhart Hauptmann from naturalism. Grillparzer and Stifter, we might say, owe less to 'Biedermeier' than 'Biedermeier', or the critics who suggested the term, owe them. Young Germany is a different matter; with its radical views it was bound to attract young writers and could possibly have launched a great talent on its career. No such towering figures can be discerned, though both Laube and Gutzkow enjoyed a long and active life. Gutzkow's novels—usually in several volumes—his comedy *Zopf und Schwert* (1844), and a drama *Uriel Acosta* (1847) demonstrate that he continued as a staunch defender of human rights, but he may well have rendered his greatest services as a mentor of young talents and editor of literary periodicals, and as co-founder of the 'Schillerstiftung'. Laube's switch from a literary to a practical life was no less pronounced and fruitful. In 1848 he was elected a member of the 'Frankfurter Nationalversammlung', and from 1849 to 1867 he was instrumental in raising the 'Burgtheater' in Vienna to its exalted place. Good playwright though he proved to be in *Struensee* (1847) and *Die Karlsschüler* (1846)—the latter a still popular dramatization of Schiller's youth—he made his most valuable contribution to artistic life as director and producer at the 'Burg'.

Eagerly read as some of the fiction of Young Germany once was, it has since become *terra incognita* even for the specialist. The long novels have never been provided with the scholarly footnotes to move into respectable company, and most of them are unavailable except in libraries. But what was clearly a transitional period qualifies as a seminal time of growing interest for the modern historian.

The advance of the technological age was no longer overlooked or dismissed as an unwelcome and passing phenomenon. The Young Germans felt that the machine had come to stay, and that a realistic literature would have to assess or even correct the economic and social consequences. The brief upheaval of the Silesian weavers in 1844 acted as a rocket which stirred emotions and prompted thoughts of redress. Robert Prutz (1816–72) in a novel, *Das Engelchen* (1851), wrote movingly of the plight of these starving people and pleaded for a humane control of industrial expansion.

Lasting gain was to accrue from Young German writers who ventured outside the German-speaking sphere to explore foreign territories. Prince Hermann von Pückler-Muskau (1785–1871), an assiduous and eccentric traveller, had in the Thirties published a number of books in which he blended his own observations with fictitious events, such as *Semilasso in Afrika* (1836). Others were to follow with a more reliable and realistic bent. Friedrich Gerstäcker (1816–72) had a first-hand knowledge of the United States and Mexico and produced in *Die Regulatoren in Arkansas* (1845) and *Die Flusspiraten des Mississippi* (1848) accounts of interest and suspense, with detailed comments on social and political mores in the frontier districts. More observer than imaginative writer, he served as an often used source of information for German novelists who required American material of a more specific kind than pre-realistic literature had been content with. Charles Sealsfield (1793–1864), who as Karl Anton Postl escaped in 1823 from a monastery in Austria and went to North America, was to become the first representative of a new literary species, the German-American writer. He wrote in English and German, and his novel *Der Legitime und die Republikaner* (1833) and the stories in *Das Cajütenbuch oder nationale Characteristiken* (1841) are no longer the hastily conceived reports of an itinerant journalist, but give the observations and reflections of one who writes from within, as a citizen of the new world. Though he was to be followed by many other immigrants who took to pen and paper, Sealsfield ranks highest among these hyphenated novelists, by virtue of a cultivated style and an intimate familiarity with American life.

Flight to North America is a thought which occurred to more than one hero of Young German novels. In 1838 Ernst Willkomm

(1810–86) picked up a general trend when he entitled one of his novels *Die Europamüden*. It is a listless account of a number of confused minds plagued by philosophical and religious scruples and hoping to find a haven across the ocean. Indirectly the book did German literature a good turn by provoking its counterpart, Ferdinand Kürnberger's (1821–79) *Der Amerika-Müde* (1855), the tale of a disgruntled and disappointed immigrant, with many details supplied by Nikolaus Lenau after his ill-fated attempt to discover an El Dorado of primeval virtues in America. But what was meant to be a warning to would-be emigrants and idealists is today a hilariously funny tale of woes befalling a misanthropic traveller, who has his own naïveté to blame for the misfortunes he experiences.

Reference has been made to the journalistic efforts of many Young Germans. Laube, Gutzkow and others, if they could not eke out a living from contributions to newspapers and magazines, nevertheless helped to develop this medium of communication. The year 1848 brought into existence a number of new periodicals and papers, and though some of them were short-lived, replacements came thick and fast. Most of them gave generous space to the *feuilleton*, either for the serialization of novels and stories or for the discussion of political and social topics. The prototype of the popular literary magazine was *Die Gartenlaube*, established in 1853. Those who remember only the declining days of this 'Familienblatt' ought to recall that it was in its better days the repository of the works of Auerbach, Spielhagen, Raabe, Storm, Fontane, Marie von Ebner-Eschenbach and other prominent writers. *Westermanns Monatshefte*, *Über Land und Meer*, *Daheim*, started publication between 1857 and 1864, and many similar periodicals were to follow in German-speaking countries. The *Deutsche Rundschau* (1874–1964) must take pride of place, as far as a high literary level is concerned.

It is unlikely that the serial publication of narrative literature had any influence on style and composition. The works were in most cases submitted in completed form meant for book production. Writing for newspapers did, on the other hand, entail considerations that bore on style. Heine, as the Parisian correspondent of the Augsburg *Allgemeine Zeitung*, is commonly regarded as the first German who came near to fulfilling the demands of excellent journalism with a missionary sense—in his case intellectual mediation between France and Germany—and his lucidity of expression and flair for entertainment. But once Ludwig Börne (1786–1837) emerges from the regrettable neglect he still suffers he may well be honoured as the initiator of German journalism. His *Briefe aus Paris* (1832–34) show him far better informed than Heine, his eagerness to enlighten the German public made him an outstanding stylist but cautioned him not to misuse his brilliant satirical gifts. Moreover, his political and social ideas kept him on a steady course of liberalism and republicanism. The freedom he fought for was for him, however, unthinkable and unobtainable without the loftiest standards of moral conduct. Heine's dislike of his compatriot and companion in exile, vented in his diatribe *Über Ludwig Börne* (1840), has sadly distorted the picture of a man to whom the Young Germans felt deeply indebted for the ideas he provided them with.

Laura Hofrichter makes Heine's journalistic engagement the revolving target that changed his outlook on life as well as his style of writing—attention to reality imparted to his work more and more of the characteristics of realistic poetry and prose. It can be assumed that other writers of this period who had their fling at journalism experienced a similar training in precision of observation and consideration for the reading public. Realism advanced on many fronts. It is this general trend which brings 'Biedermeier' and Young Germany together, regardless of their other differences. If the representatives of 'Biedermeier' practised the realism of minute and affectionate description in their private sphere, the Young Germans were, or tried to become, more realistic in their political and social thinking than the advocates of restoration could afford to be. The confluence of these two streams of realism was to result, in the second half of the century, in a number of works in which an objective rendering of a fondly viewed outside world combines with a clear recognition of the need for shouldering social obligations to the masses. The instinctively felt solidarity with all mankind, which together with the concomitant movement towards realism we hold to be the hallmark of nineteenth-century literature, is implicitly contained in and furthered by both 'Biedermeier' and Young German writing.

Some historians, to bolster the literary achievements of Young

Germany, number Christian Dietrich Grabbe (1801–36) and
Georg Büchner (1813–37) among its adherents. We prefer to
treat them as outsiders with only the most tenuous connection with
the political optimism of their period. It is natural that in the partly
idyllic and partly febrile years between 1815 and 1848 a few talents
would see their chance to storm into literature—rather than into
politics—with ostentatious self-confidence and an utter disregard
for literary traditions. Such courage seemed to augur particularly
well for the rejuvenation of drama. Grabbe dismissed both Goethe
and Schiller as pitifully passé. He was one of those writers whom we
mentioned as unwilling to wait for the second part of *Faust*, and so,
his imagination and above all his ambition sparked by Byron's
Manfred and *Cain*, he went to work on a *Don Juan und Faust* tragedy
(1829), a dangerous act on the literary flying trapeze which resulted
in an unfortunate hybrid, revealing at best a seam between the two
motifs and at its worst a crack down the middle of the play. There
is a reckless boldness in this attempt to make Faust, the embodiment
of insatiable intellectual curiosity, compete with Don Juan, the
never-satisfied lover, for the favours of one and the same Donna
Anna. With all its frenzied scenes and confrontations the play
revolves around an insight that is now a commonplace: erotic
drives and lust for power are basic promptings. Grabbe anticipates
both Freud and Adler, but is no more successful in making one out
of the two than the two Viennese psychologists were in becoming
of one mind. Much as we admire Grabbe's power to embroil his
characters in two passions, for knowledge, and for women, we
wonder whether the idea of a German metaphysician and a Spanish
hidalgo running after the same girl would not have served better
for a comedy. German audiences thought differently. This monumental polarization of two massive instincts was Grabbe's most
successful play in his lifetime, and between 1870 and 1890 it recap-
tured the German stage once more. Its overheated characters, closer
to Wagner than to Hauptmann, and better suited to singing arias
than speaking in blank verse, were again able to deceive people into
believing that a burning theme was being enacted, the clash between
knowledge and faith, and between body and soul. But alas, times
had changed, the hour had now come to let the Silesian weavers
speak, or to have somebody speak for them. True enough, Grabbe's

Faust raises a point which we experience as a truly existential problem: you cannot believe unless you know, and you cannot know unless you believe; and there are other passages to illumine the dilemma of man. The pity of it is that Grabbe lost so much of his modernity in his dramatic implementation, by staging the conflicts after the manner of shouting matches on the operatic stage and with characters pretending to be supermen. But, eager to find his own dramatic style—the polish of classical drama being unsuited for his drastic, irreverent way of thinking—he was apt to be loud rather than subtle. He did better in his comedy *Scherz, Satire, Ironie und tiefere Bedeutung* (1827) and in his historical plays, *Napoleon oder die hundert Tage* (1831) and *Hannibal* (1835). Recent performances of the comedy were bound to surprise those who thought the theatre of the absurd to be the *dernier cri* in avant-gardism. The play is an intriguing web of fancy, wit, and nonsense that seems to draw together Nestroy and Beckett; what is most gratifying is that its absurd characters and situations do become, as the title suggests, translucent for some kind of deeper significance, exposing as they do the wretchedness of ignorance and pedantry, of arrogance and stupidity, and extolling the appeal of true poetry. Yet nowhere do we feel the heavy hand of German polemics; the scenes are so many delightful explosions into humour, satire and reflection. They teach nothing and imbue the spectator with serenity and thus form an early antidote to the malaise and anxiety of a later time.

Napoleon oder die hundert Tage is easily Grabbe's most interesting work, for both psychological and formal reasons. It reverberates the mental conflicts of the restoration. Depressed by the lethargy of the period and its lack of progressive aims, and in order to stir things up, Grabbe conjures up Napoleon, to provoke action and mobilize energies. But on closer inspection and when examining the returning hero and 'Weltgeist' the author, with the realistic outlook of the younger generation, discovers that the great man is most likely a myth and certainly not needed for the well-being of mankind. The titan is best thrown into the dustbin of history. Grabbe nowhere comes near the satirical re-examination of history in which Shaw was to excel. We respect his restraint, for he tries hard to distil some meaning out of the broth of events, preferably a movement towards greater justice and equality. His efforts are of little avail, however, and the drama ends inconclusively. On the one hand Grabbe treats Napoleon's last appearance on the European scene as a significant event in history, or more specifically as another crisis in the unfinished French revolution. The latter must be credited with having given rise to a more insistent demand for freedom, within France and without. The victory of liberty over tyrants makes sense and is a progressive step, and so there was no place for a returning Napoleon. But what are we to think of the fact that the victorious people were again enslaved by the new rulers who refused to redeem the promises given to their soldiers? Grabbe regretfully alludes to this betrayal, and there the matter rests. We cannot rely on the progressive march of history, and Grabbe with the very realism of his psychological and sociological method leads us to the conclusion that we had better forgo all hopes for the advancement of society. As for himself, he is content with a grand-stand seat to watch the thrilling but pointless spectacle of history.

If Grabbe was too independent an observer to take refuge under the Hegelian structure of history he was equally consistent in rejecting traditional forms of drama. We feel how he must have been tempted to revert to the grand style of drama—with Napoleon approaching like a thunderstorm and the French, most of them, expecting a welcome cleansing of the atmosphere! The events seem to be set to proceed in accordance with the form and requirements of classical drama: high expectations at first, and in the end an inexorable fate entering the stage at Waterloo. But reality, as Grabbe sees it, plotted a different course. His citizens of Paris do not act and react in the idealistic manner of conventional drama, they turn out to be individuals who have their different ways of judging things, patriotically and indifferently, sentimentally and cynically. In order to give as objective a spectrum of public opinion as possible, Grabbe breaks up his play into a number of short scenes, each of which contributes its own striking colour to the total picture. The refraction in different minds of one and the same event, the return of Napoleon, makes history a puzzling phenomenon and requires a mixture of styles and moods, epic and dramatic, sadness and relief. Every onlooker and commentator has his own way of judging a historic event: anchored in his personality, we are treated to a kaleidoscopic round of opinions and evaluations and receive a confusing if not nihilistic interpretation of reality.

But for the appearance of George Büchner we should probably attribute some of the technical novelties in the plays of Wedekind, Hauptmann, and Brecht to Grabbe. As it is, we have the exact date of Büchner's impact, 1913, when the fragment of his tragedy *Woyzeck*, discovered in 1879, saw its first performance. Again it was the composition of this work, short scenes without any grouping into acts, that accounted for the appeal and helped in the liberation from traditional structures of drama. What was gained was a sharp focusing on essential confrontations and swiftly changing scenes, with no need to provide pedantically for connecting links.

In 1913 it was the style of Büchner's drama that attracted attention—after the Second World War it is the pessimistic element in his works which leaves us wondering about the logic of literary developments. How is the appearance of such a sombre outlook, so out of place in the optimism of the nineteenth century, to be explained? Fear and despair can rise at all times, and the years after the Napoleonic wars, with exhaustion, confusion or resignation following the collective efforts of liberation, may well have affected younger people depressively. Also, we must not forget that Schopenhauer's first volume of *Die Welt als Wille und Vorstellung* appeared in 1819 and that *Die Nachtwachen des Bonaventura* (1804), a compendium of all the horrors life can have in store, was variously attributed to E. T. A. Hoffmann, Jean Paul, Schelling, Friedrich Schlegel—all considered capable of such bottomless despair. But while these are works that commented more theoretically and almost elegantly on the bungled job that God's creation is, Grabbe, and to an even greater degree Büchner, communicate a *taedium vitae* that chills the bones before it reaches the brain. Generally speaking, the forces of faith were time and again able to close ranks and keep out serious misgivings concerning a purposeful, progressive civilization, but subterranean currents of doubt became, as we have said, nevertheless noticeable.

In Büchner this pessimism comes right to the surface; his creative work is filled with it, much to the consternation of those who claim him, as the author of *Der Hessische Landbote* (1834), for the cause of socialism. This manifesto sounded indeed like a clarion call to revolution. A cold enumeration, seemingly factually compiled but exuding all the political passion of a rebel, of the many abuses perpetrated by the Hessian government, is interspersed with demands for and threats of revolutionary remedies. Moreover, we know that Büchner was associated with a group of social radicals. The *Landbote* made him and his friends suspicious elements, and he escaped incarceration and worse by moving to Strasbourg, where he was out of reach of the German police. All these facts point in the direction of a budding socialist writer, a follower of Young Germany who might surpass all the other adherents in devotion to radical activism. But nothing of the sort happened, the revolutionary fervour freezes, in Büchner's literary creations, into scepticism and despair. The contrast and shock come with greatest force in *Dantons Tod* (1835), in this anatomy of the most decisive revolution, which turns into an exposure of its wanton cruelty and inherently unattainable aims.

Woyzeck, it is true, was for a long time accepted by the critics and the theatre-goers as strong evidence of Büchner's sympathy with the underdog. The play about the hapless soldier whose paramour betrays him with an ebullient drum-major and provokes him to murder her and to commit suicide was long regarded as one of the great events in German social drama, the step down to the proletariat, after the eighteenth century had declared the middle-classes fit material for tragic consumption and human sympathy. As Elise Dosenheimer puts it: "Twenty-five years before the appearance of Marx a young poet by dramatizing the fate of a poor, inconspicuous individual turns prophet and makes drama a mene tekel: economic conditions are in the process of playing fate or at any rate co-operating with fate.'

There is no doubt that Woyzeck is being victimized by society. In order to supplement his wages he does odd jobs for his superiors and earns a few extra pennies by acting as a guinea-pig for a doctor and self-styled scientist. He is conscious of his poverty. 'I think that if we poor people go to heaven we shall have to help producing thunder.' We are willing to concede that but for his constant worrying about his common-law wife and an illegitimate child Woyzeck might live more intelligently and avert tragedy. But with greater empathy we sense a deeper than economic cause of his misery. Woyzeck seems to be a really tragic figure, one which, in the words of Hebbel, would not have been saved by a full purse. It is not only

B

the poor man, but Everyman that stands here exposed in his help-lessness, a victim not just of social accident, but of an existential predicament, an outcry for the whole of mankind, a question mark for all that exists and suffers: why do we have to live and what for? The particular misery of Woyzeck makes life as such questionable and evokes a pity that spills over to all living beings. The horror is the more shocking, when we realize how close Woyzeck seems to have come to the fulfilment of his yearning for happiness. Life could be so beautiful, with a full-blooded woman like Marie and a normal little child around! A chance meeting with the drum-major, and Marie slips out of his hands. What fragile stuff life is made of! Even at its best it can only provide material for a comedy such as *Leonce und Lena* (1836), a chess-play of boredom in sophisticated high society, with never a breeze of vitality and purpose to blow away its ennui. Whatever Büchner touches seems to congeal into anxiety, fear, death. Or is it because he reaches for characters and plots which contain the seed of self-destruction in them? In the one short story he wrote, *Lenz* (published in 1839), named after the un-fortunate German poet and erstwhile boon companion of Goethe at Strasbourg, Büchner takes over this mental patient at a time when he is already a hopeless case of schizophrenia, wandering aimlessly about and being cared for by kind-hearted people, until confine-ment to an institution becomes necessary. 'Lenz is the sort of hero whose existence outgrows, almost threatens, his author,' J. P. Stern says in his searching essay on Büchner. Indeed, the power of insight and sympathy is congenital enough to make us wonder whether Büchner's escape into science would have saved him from himself. Whether it be the half-witted Woyzeck or the near-genius Lenz, Büchner must take them on the road to despair and doom.

By comparison, such despair in *Dantons Tod* is well accounted for. It seems to stem as much from man's follies, from his madness in trying to legislate for a millennium for society, as from existential conditions. Danton's abysmal boredom is more the result of his life than of existence as such, though he naturally starts to rationalize and puts the blame on Him who is responsible for the creation of the world. But this is to happen later. We see him first simply tired of revolutionary activities, and of the vocabulary of the activists. As a private citizen he could just stop using their highfalutin words, keep quiet about his misgivings and look scornfully at the continued demagogy of the others, but as a former ringleader of the revolution he is bound to clash head on with Robespierre, Saint-Just and their henchmen, all inebriated with the phraseology of world-saviours. Danton cannot simply change over to his own sweet hedonistic way, much as he now believes that pleasure is the only true vocation of man and enjoyment of life the finest form of prayer. He is dragging the past with him; memories of the September murders, whose instigator he was, haunt him by day and night and cannot be assuaged by his wife's reassurance that he had to be cruel in order to save the country. As if saving the country were not another of these empty phrases he has come to detest. It is a foregone conclusion that Danton will lose his last bout with Robespierre, first because he refuses to believe that the opposition will ever dare to stage a trial against him, second because he is in no mood to fight back, and third because basically he yearns for death or, to be more accurate, for complete annihilation. The Sophoclean lament that it would be best not to be born echoes in many forms in Danton's conversations.

It goes without saying that one so deeply tortured by the paradox between an existence which pleasure alone can justify and a world which treats us only to misery, one so thoroughly imbued with the desire for absolute oblivion, must balk at the ideologists and activists who engage in human engineering on the grandest scale and regard the liquidation of thousands of people as a necessary and pardonable correction on the road to the millennium. The conflict is between the mad activism of Robespierre, and even more of Saint-Just, and a passivity of the most lethargic kind. It is understandable that in the presence of such monstrous planners who, like Saint-Just, invoke the laws of nature, or its catastrophes, earthquakes and floods, to defend violent interference with human society, a sensitive soul can be driven to the other extreme of wishing for death and nothingness. To contemplate such an escape is to concede victory to the brutalizing forces, and since the play does not give the slightest hint that the transgressors against all humanity and, incidentally, also the murderers of Danton and his friends, are to meet the same fate, Büchner leaves us no middle road to walk and no normal people to point the way to hope and progress. There is no prospect of reason-

able forces taking matters in hand and rebuilding on a better foundation. The question that worries Danton to the last minute of his
life—whether there will be final dissolution and release from the
compulsion to live—remains unanswered; there is no comfort to be
drawn from this side either. We are however not left in doubt concerning the quality of the life to which we seem to be condemned—
it is absurd and more often worse. We cannot, as some critics do,
take the last scene of the play, where Lucile, Camille Desmoulins'
widow, provokes her arrest and execution, as evidence of a faint
stirring of human dignity and free will that redeem life. The feeling
of a blind and cruel fate is not lifted; there is nothing to live for and
no way to cancel this cosmic mistake—existence. If there is a spark
of human greatness in the play, or of hope for mankind, it is Danton's
resolution to dissociate himself from the social and political quacks;
with some goodwill we can date his pessimistic leanings from the
time when he begins to perceive the monstrous cure he and his
fellow-revolutionaries had prescribed for France, or when reason
and compassion surge back into his mind and heart.

The unmitigated condemnation of being, as well as the strong
verdict against brutal interference with the life of society, has made
Dantons Tod palpitatingly attractive for modern readers and stage-
directors. The play is the expression of total pessimism or at the
very least of total pessimism with regard to any radical cures for
social and political ills. It invalidates the placing of Büchner among
the early socialists. Danton recants the message of *Der Hessische
Landbote*. The prophet of gloom and exponent of existential 'Angst'
can be in no mood to stir us into political motion. J. P. Stern

evolves as the central theme and concern of Büchner's life and work
the reality of suffering and its meaning for man. Of its reality we are
easily convinced. But what about its meaning? Stern finds the answer
in Lenz, whose ability to suffer provides him with a last contact with
reality, while from the time he ceases to suffer 'he has relinquished
his hold upon our world'. Suffering then is the ransom we pay to
stay alive and real, the price we have to give if we want to experience the distinctiveness of our existence. On his death-bed Büchner
is reported to have spoken these last words to a friend: 'Wir haben
der Schmerzen nicht zuviel, wir haben ihrer zu wenig, denn durch
den Schmerz gehen wir zu Gott ein.' This may, as a German critic

has said, ask for a theological interpretation of Büchner's writings. We do not get very far with this approach, and even Stern, who has a good ear for religious overtones, ventures no theological conclusions and retreats to the existential situation—pain is the medium through which we apprehend the world, it is through pain that, paradoxically enough, the surpassing beauty of the world can be glimpsed, if only in rare moments. But the latter will suffice to goad us on and to make life a coveted goal. We are, of course, reminded of Schopenhauer's incessant demonstrations of how the will to live tricks us into its service, without ever fulfilling the expectations held dangling before us. Yet for Büchner the splendour of existence seems to be a real possibility. 'What a wonderful girl she was!' Woyzeck can say of his love and victim Marie, and the expression and its context make this a truth felt with his whole existence—it needs only a stroke of luck, and life could be an immensely saturating bliss.

Whatever intents and ideas we read into Büchner's work, he is clearly one of the great writers and poets who by the very language and composition of their creations can evoke a vibrating resonance to life, though preponderantly to its horror, mystery and deceptiveness. While different times have heard different messages, social, existential and theological, the fascination issuing from the form of his plays, most emphatically from *Woyzeck*, has affected and is still affecting German playwrights. *Dantons Tod* strikes one as being more closely hewn to traditional form. Some of its innovations had been introduced before, such as an almost verbatim montage of revolutionary oratory recorded in the historical documents, a swift change of scenes taking us from the drawing-rooms and assembly halls to the streets of Paris, yet all of them contributing to a claustrophobic feeling of time and space closing in on Danton and his friends, until they are all in prison and have only one exit left, the guillotine. The double service rendered by some of these scenes, as 'Stimmungsbild' and dramatic propulsion, gives the play a compactness far surpassing that which his imitators of the 'Stationen' technique were able to achieve. But it is in *Woyzeck* that we find a new style of drama, an inspiration, as we said, for dramatists ever since its first performance, though it must be doubted that any of them achieved so much with what seems so little in the way of language and composition. A number of brief scenes, each marked by a dense atmosphere, literally hunt their victim and drive the sweat out of his pores. The plot can be guessed once we have seen and heard the braggart of a drum-major, an explosion of conceit and arrogance, sexual erection verbalized; the course of the action from then on is commonplace, and the dramatist is free to make it replete with anxiety, with horrible premonition accompanied but not relieved by comic interludes. How is it all achieved? The life of the play issues from the word, and often from the absence of words; for it is as if the pressure from all sides, from a drab reality, from haunting superstition or sheer despair, makes Woyzeck forget what little grammar he has. He begins to stutter or falls silent and is driven to the language of gestures, only to make the predicament of his and of all human existence more poignantly clear. Incoherent phrases provide the intermediate links for what is going on, outside of Woyzeck and particularly within. He speaks, as Stern says, in sentences which 'are discontinuous as his self is isolated'.

In *Dantons Tod* such isolation is as much commented on as it is vividly felt and painfully endured. 'Wir wissen wenig voneinander,' Danton resignedly states in the very first scene. Though he and others go on talking and deliberating with one another, the common bond is mainly that of suffering and despair, and the futile wish for concerted action. Similarly *Woyzeck* transposes us into a world in which pain and disappointment stand out as the preponderant realities. Unless we draw comfort from the fact that a number of queer and dehumanized characters seem to be able to live impervious to the horror of existence, or unless we take our place among the children who in excited curiosity rush out to the scene where Marie was murdered, or unless we identify ourselves with the professional joy of a policeman—'as beautiful a murder as one could hope for. Not in a long time have we had one like that'—we have nothing to look forward to in Büchner's world, not even to Oberlin, the great humanitarian who befriends Lenz without being able to help him.

But to repeat: the thought of a life that is wholly superfluous, a cruel role assigned to us by an unfeeling God, had its expounders before and after Büchner. What was new and not to be paralleled for a long time is the immediate apprehension of our existential predicament which Büchner inflicts. Naturalism and expressionism have unsparingly forced us to see the festering wounds caused by social indifference and wars, but they did so with the implicit assumption that if we were but to obey the promptings of our hearts life would become bearable for all. As to the modern prophets of gloom and fear, they often either fail to express what they feel or to feel what they express.

4 *Problematic Writers*

The events of 1848 discouraged the Young Germans but lifted the pall of timidity hanging over 'Biedermeier'. On balance the atmosphere was favourable to intellectual and even more to artistic pursuits, as long as these kept within the bounds set by mildly liberal, but still right-of-centre, authorities. The lull in activist literary movements, enforced or voluntarily accepted, may well have been conducive to a more careful craftsmanship and have led to a more searching consideration of artistic standards. It is in the Fifties that a number of writers make their début with undisputed masterpieces or reach the zenith of their careers. Literary historians, as we have indicated, are fond of discussing the period from the middle of the century to its end as the age of bourgeois realism. To avoid such over-simplification we propose to see and describe three major forces which seem to make up the bulk of nineteenth-century writing even before 1848: peasant literature, bourgeois literature and Austrian writing. To these three mythologies, as we might call them, must be added a fourth one, though its flourishing came at a later time: marxist or socialistic literature.

We cannot establish such a classification without at once admitting the existence of many outsiders, just as Grabbe and Büchner were outsiders to Young Germany. 'Trivialliteratur', easily as most of it could be tucked in with the three groups, will be left out of consideration. But at the other end of the scale we have a series of writers who became so embedded in philosophical thought or in questions of aesthetic presentation that they lost or spurned contact with the ordinary reader and common man—a contact which makes bourgeois and peasant writing and Austrian literature a basically popular form of writing—though this is not to imply that they lack intellectual vigour. We have mentioned before that the heritage of classicism and romanticism, with its roots in the ancient world and in Shakespeare and the Spanish Golden Age, was very much in the consciousness of nineteenth-century writers. Grillparzer, Stifter, Keller, Ludwig, Storm, and Fontane can all hold their own in theor-

etical discussions on literature; Freytag and Spielhagen wrote under-
standingly on the theory of the novel and the drama, and Otto
Ludwig must be regarded as one of the more profound analysts of
literature. But such studies and knowledge of aesthetic theory served
them in a subsidiary capacity, by helping them to develop their
craft. Concerned with society, they preferred to question life rather
than philosophy, to write of people rather than to speculate on aesthe-
tics. The end of classical philosophy, which according to Georg
Lukács came with Feuerbach, was followed by a vigorously thriving
narrative art, as if spiritual guidance, after having first passed from
the priest to the philosopher, was now to be provided by the writer.

There is in the relationship of the outsider type to the other
writers something of the nexus between pure scientists and applied
scientists, without any feeling of superiority on either side, because
there is an uninterrupted flow of influence in both directions. A
formalist of the distinction of August Graf von Platen (1796–1835)
did much to keep alive the feeling for exquisitely wrought verse,
and a thinker like Friedrich Hebbel owes much to the contemporary
popular literature which he so avidly read. But it was never just
give or take, but always both.

Friedrich Hebbel (1813–63) seemed to have been predestined to
leave his mark on a realistic literature with pronounced social
leanings. Born in poor surroundings, exploited by those who
recognized his precocious abilities, unable to get more than a scanty
primary education and forced to undergo great privations to make
possible an irregular attendance at the universities of Erlangen and
Munich, the boy collected on his way to manhood all the experiences that so often form into a strong social protest. Nor did time
blunt his recollections or dull the sharpness of his resentment. Yet
in spite of it all he so moulded his personality that it became most
of all an instrument for a relentless philosophical curiosity. He
resembles Nietzsche in many ways, not least because he too allowed
a broader experience of life to be subjugated by his concern with
aesthetic, metaphysical and existential problems. What might have
formed his chief endeavour, the literary exploitation of what he had
suffered, appears only sporadically in the odd, oblique curse on his
tormentors. Even his early tragedy *Maria Magdalene* (1844), commonly referred to as a social drama, does not really take issue with

man's inhumanity to man, but rather attempts to see social conditions, however deplorable, in the context of historical and philosophical necessity, and even to condone them.

Instead of voicing his protest and becoming a realist in his art and a socialist in his thinking Hebbel bent his efforts towards a drama that would lead the classical tradition to new heights of perfection. For though he had the assiduous and searching mind of Otto Ludwig in studying literary models, he was able to involve and control such knowledge in a genuinely personal act of creativeness. With him classical drama performed for the last time with all its technical brilliance and profound ideas. There comes, after Hebbel, an interregnum of insignificant theatrical literature, a stop-gap until the arrival of the naturalists in the early Nineties. Now the only way in which the classical tradition could be creatively resumed was by assigning to it a timeless function, which would enable it to reveal yet other hitherto undiscovered truths. Hebbel made this clear in his 'Vorwort' to *Maria Magdalene* with some borrowing from dialectic philosophy. He states that while the most signal changes in the march of civilization belong to the past—in his own plays they were to appear mainly as the transition from a pagan to a Christian era—there is still something left for us: 'to prepare a better foundation for such institutions as we have and to base them on a morality and necessity that are in fact identical'. It is a pity that in his own work, with the possible exception of *Maria Magdalene*, he did not trace the still untrodden paths to such corrections in our civilization, but preferred, as we said, to re-enact the violent upheavals of an earlier time. Trying to pronounce on future developments, apart from requiring a clairvoyance he did not have, might have shaken his belief in the serviceability of the classical forms. Given his mastery of the essential structure of classical drama he found it easier to operate with historically authenticated ideas that responded to his highly artistic and precisely calculated, though basically derivative, forms. Moreover, there is a strong possibility that Hebbel's exploratory advance into the future was blocked by insecurity and doubt. He confided these doubts to his letters and diaries, while as a playwright he presents a world of meaningful decisions and soul-filling tasks—or so they must have appeared at some time in the distant past.

His first play *Judith* (1841) shows him at the cross-roads and trying both directions—the subject is taken from biblical history, the treatment he gives it is highly original. It was more than anything his psychology that seemed to mark a bold advance over the customary concept of human motivation. Both courage and tact were required to make a woman the only manly person in the town of Bethulia beleaguered by Holofernes and debilitated by thirst, hunger, and fear, without at the same time coarsening Judith's feminine traits. It was even more difficult to bring her back from an excursion into patriotic murder not as a puffed-up heroine, but as a woman tortured by inner turmoil, with a mind which overnight had turned into a cruelly sensitive instrument, unwilling to receive the acclaim of her people and to be fêted as their saviour. What happened is, seen from a first level of interpretation, simply this: bravely though naïvely she goes over into the camp of Holofernes, bent on killing him for the deliverance of the town. On meeting Holofernes she experiences the disgust and hatred she is prepared for, but she also feels intermittent admiration and attraction. When, after the murder, hate prevails again, it is no longer the hatred of the patriot for a deadly enemy, but the more poignant aversion of a woman who surrendered to an irresistible man without being made to feel that he cared for her more than as an attractive body. This explanation seems to say all and to give a good measure of Hebbel's subtle psychology.

But this is only a beginning, with more interpretative complications to come. If Judith completed her murderous mission not for the sake of her people and for the glory of God, but in order to revenge her outraged womanhood, is it not then permissible to assume that she should feel deserted by God, tricked into a humiliating experience, bitter enough to plunge her into a despair bordering on tragedy? Hebbel in his diaries threw out another hint as to the source of tragedy in his play. God has to punish murder even where he must have welcomed, commissioned it, as in Judith's case. Nemesis there must be, and it comes with the possibility, dreaded by Judith, that she may have to bear a son of Holofernes. God's instrument is inwardly crushed, because he allowed it to become morally guilty. God uses us as a tool for his intentions, but like a coward he withholds his support when in the act of carrying out his orders we become guilty of some crime. What kind of a God is this who demands that we expiate a trespass we have committed at his instigation? To make matters slightly more complex it has been suggested that Judith's crime is not so much the deed of an outraged woman, but the killing of a man she loved. The two should have lived happily ever after their nuptial embrace. The crux of the matter is that, far-fetched as some of these views appear to be, Judith's behaviour after her return complies with and justifies any of these interpretations, including that of a Judith who feels tragically wounded because she has implicated God in her crime, by not carrying out his orders with the purity he expected her to retain. If all this is an indication of how difficult Hebbel can make it, without perhaps wanting to, for his readers to unravel the tangle of motives, things become much worse when he deliberately explores and brings into interplay the complications of human relationships. His razor-sharp mind can split a thread of action into many filaments, to weave them expertly together again. The memory and intelligence of an audience are at times taxed beyond a bearable limit, and, with all its intricate conflicts and swiftly succeeding confrontations, a work like *Ein Trauerspiel in Sizilien* (1847) begs to be treated as a 'Lesedrama' or watched like a fast-moving chess game. Yet Hebbel thought very highly of this play.

The same astonishing mental power enabled Hebbel to plan and construct most effective drama, starting with an exposition that is charged with references to coming events which will then unfold with machine-like precision. Better still, he can envelop his coldly planned structures in an aura of lyricism which now and then simulates the emotional warmth and the symbolic language of the intuitive poet. Schiller's 'sentimentalischer Dichter' striving to look naïve has nowhere better succeeded than with Hebbel. The harder he thought about the nature of drama and the essence of tragedy the better he managed to illustrate his theories. This is truer of *Maria Magdalene* than of *Genoveva* (1843) and *Der Diamant* (1847). For with *Maria Magdalene* he made bold to put the philosophical reflections of the preface to the play on stage, and as Edna Purdie says: '. . . the drama of *Maria Magdalene* vindicates the artist in Hebbel from the philosophic critic.' The philosophical accoutrements, greatly indebted to Hegel, are briefly these: Progress or even the mere survival of men requires continuous changes; a given social, political or cultural situation may outlive its usefulness and deteriorate into a status quo which in time will provoke its antithesis, a set of new ideas and convictions leading to a restored equilibrium between old and new, until this synthesis in turn assumes all the weary symptoms of a thesis calling for another remedial or rebellious antithesis. These dialectic spurts and fits are, of course, carried out by human beings, and it can easily happen that the man with some bold antithetical thinking, marching in the front line of new thoughts and feelings, pays with his life for his trail-blazing. With reference to such imperilled pioneers Hebbel could speak of the pantragic aspect of life.

If the formal features of this philosophy of history made it easy for him to define the tragic victim, it was considerably more difficult to pattern the dialectic process with the figures of human beings acting in some particular time and place, under historical compulsion. The best demonstration Hebbel found in such a 'Wendezeit' as the transition from paganism to Christianity. But what other transitions can be detected within the large time-spans before or after? Here the changes were more minute, of a social nature, for instance the break-up of patriarchical modes of social organization. They would still be a noticeable adjustment of universal or at any rate of national dimensions. Its reverberations might be felt high and low, and what happened somewhere could well indicate what happened anywhere. 'It is irrelevant whether the hand of the clock is made of gold or of brass, and it does not matter whether a significant symbolic action takes place on a lower or higher social level.'

Maria Magdalene is the tragedy of a modest middle-class milieu, the hand of the clock consists of base metal, but it moves with precision to tell us that the historic hour has struck. The rules and regulations governing middle-class behaviour, much as they may once have helped to secure more freedom for development, have become obsolete in the middle of the nineteenth century, and begin to stifle expanding energies. Meister Anton, the paterfamilias, an honest, hard working cabinet-maker and within limits a kind man— though it is he himself who has to reveal the good turns he has done to some of his friends—sees the world of probity and parental authority collapsing. His son frequents the bowling alleys, a good enough reason for the father to contend that the boy is a good-for-nothing, and to believe, erroneously, as it turns out, that he is a thief. With half of the family reputation seemingly gone, he clings to his daughter Klara, if only to tell her that he would cut his throat, if she too should dishonour him. This is, of course, what she is in a fair way to do, finding herself pregnant and jilted by her fiancé in a cruel game of human relationships. The choice between suicide or driving her father to kill himself is quickly made, and all that remains is for Klara to simulate an accident, and for the father to insist that it was one and to squash rumours to the contrary. In the end one of the characters has the guts to tell Anton off and to unmask his murderous righteousness for what it is, a frantic attempt to present the façade of a good middle-class home. Anton with one last stiffening of his hardness and hollowness, partly excusing himself and partly shifting the blame, exclaims: 'Ich verstehe die Welt nicht mehr.' Those in the play who dimly do understand that the world is changing are either too late with their insight or too eager to dissociate themselves from outworn modes of living. But all seem to be, as Edna Purdie puts it, 'more than usually dependent upon their environment, more than usually powerless to free themselves from its control'. In this denial of free will, good or evil, the villain of the play, Leonhard, who withdraws on hearing that Klara's brother is suspected of theft and that the father has given away her dowry to help some poor fellow, must also be excused. He had to look after his career as a smart young clerk, and the laws of supply and demand force him to elbow his way into a secure and remunerative position.

The incisiveness of the language and the compactness of the events, with hardly a word or a gesture that does not interrelate the past with the present and allude to the future, are almost overdone. We have the impression of a machine chopping off the head of anyone who comes too close to it. But again the same sharp intellect devises means to counteract the effect of an all too conscious arrangement. Change as the essence of life is unobtrusively woven into the fabric of the play, as when somebody comments on the difference in fashions or casually remarks on progress in education, now that everybody can read and write. The whole text, not just the plot, is impregnated with the philosophy Hebbel wants to expound. It has long been noticed that the final constriction of the play to coffins and graves and to Meister Anton's incarceration in his confined self is brought to sensuous awareness by a vocabulary and imagery making recurring references to narrowing space.

The designation of social drama, often applied to *Maria Magdalene*, is in need of qualification, whether we compare the play with Lessing's *Emilia Galotti*, Schiller's *Kabale und Liebe* or Hauptmann's *Die Weber*. The connotation at the start of this series is of class differences interfering with the voice of heart and reason, at the end that of our conscience being awakened to the plight of the lower classes. Hebbel does not come in at either side. Tragedy arises from a society suffocating within its own ideals and prejudices; it happens to be a well-defined lower bourgeois society, but its predicament can become the predicament of any class. The staleness and stuffiness of the milieu, not its head-on clash with some lower or higher class, contain and breed the tragic elements—it is in this specific sense that we can range *Maria Magdalene* among the few outstanding German social plays. It has, erroneously, it would appear, been said that Hebbel was now close enough to the social concerns of his time to become a social critic and defender of the rights of the lower classes. There is no such promise in *Maria Magdalene* nor in any other of his works. His own experience as a victim of exploitation did not, as we mentioned, goad him on to the path of the social reformer. His philosophy of history, the dialectic process manifesting itself in the categories of change, gave him no clues as to the next steps historical necessity would take. His vision, like that of his master Hegel, was obstructed by the thought that the last great antithesis had occurred years ago, with the coming of Christianity, and certainly not later than with the Reformation. *Herodes und Mariamne* (1848) and *Gyges und sein Ring* (1854) are set in ancient times, *Agnes Bernauer* (1851) and *Die Nibelungen* (1860) at the threshold of great upheavals in Germany. The significant changes coming with Christianity are for Hebbel of a very inward kind—it was most of all the new dignity of women, who had hitherto been held in subjugation, which marked for him the new era. Herodes, before leaving for war, wants to extract from his wife Mariamne the promise to kill herself if he should not return. Her self-respect forbids her to give such a promise—she would of her own free will take the course of action her husband tries to force on her. By a complicated play of moves and counter-moves Mariamne becomes almost provocative in her insistence on freedom of action, Herodes is compelled to take measures that must hurt her deeply in spite of, or because of, his love for her and which finally end in ordering her execution. Professor Purdie calls the tragedy enacted in this play 'the most modern in its problem', with two characters destroying each other by a most unreasonable show of individuality and possessiveness. 'The tragic guilt is once more that of "Unmässigkeit"—both Herodes and Mariamne are guilty in this sense, but the first, greater crime must be charged to Herodes.' One may well ask whether Hebbel, in complicating matters so much and making the psychological grating of one person on another such a torture, did not lose sight of the original purpose, which must have been to make Mariamne the herald of better times to come, of Christian respect for the rights of the individual. *Gyges und sein Ring* leads us down a similar path of self-destruction through over-sensitive reactions which all but becloud the basic issue, the overdue change from ancient rigidity to less constricted mores. King Kandaules rightly brags about the beauty of his wife, and to convince his doubting young guest from Greece, Gyges, he slips a magic ring on his finger, for an invisible inspection of Rhodope's bedroom. Something goes wrong, the queen is first suspicious and then certain that she has been violated, treated as a mere thing, as a show-piece. Kandaules, for his display of what are really easy-going, more liberal manners, has to fight a duel with his friend Gyges, since there must be one man only to set eyes on Rhodope's body, namely her husband. Gyges, much to his annoyance, fells Kandaules, but without any benefit for either himself or Rhodope—as soon as Gyges has been married to Rhodope, she drives a dagger into her heart, to restore her sense of purity. Hebbel has equipped his characters with the usual brilliant argumentation and given the downward movement the semblance of inevitability. However, technical and stylistic excellence lays bare rather than hides the mathematical calculatedness of the plot. It is difficult to equate this dialectic process with a 'Wendepunkt' in the course of civilization. If Rhodope represents the progressive turn towards a more dignified regard for women, she is at the same time a conservative and retarding force, insisting on taboos that have outlived their usefulness. Kandaules is much more enlightened, not to say modern, sceptical of tribal taboos and good-natured enough to let Gyges have his fun. He exhales a mood of conviviality, and experiments with a form of conduct that points in the direction of comedy—and one sees no reason why the collision of thesis with antithesis should not on occasion resolve itself in a merry synthesis. The story of the *Nibelungen* served Hebbel much better in showing the great divide between Teutonic paganism and the dawn of the Christian era, with its mildness and forgiveness, and though as a dramatist he is partial to the undiluted colours of primitive force, courage and loyalty—his earlier portrayal of Holofernes reveals what imaginative power she had for creating an unbroken brutal personality—the morning of a more tolerant and refined age comes with tender hues and shades as something the world was yearning for. Yet there is a lingering feeling that Hebbel's sympathy is on the side of the strong unbending characters— if not for reasons of political conservatism then because better drama can be extracted from them.

Agnes Bernauer is evidence to this effect. Duke Albrecht, heir to the Bavarian throne, falls in love with Agnes Bernauer, the daughter of an Augsburg barber, who had already become a legendary figure, entering folklore as the angel of Augsburg. Albrecht brushes all the objections and well-meant warnings of his friends aside, ready to face the implacable opposition of his father, Duke Ernst. Albrecht believes with the sincerity of a Schillerean hero in the right of the heart to determine the choice of our partner in life, and in his enthusiasm he is certain, as all young idealists are, that the trend of things points in the direction of his inclinations, in this case towards democratic ideas. What he does, so he proclaims, will set an example of progressive feeling and living and voice a protest against stale custom. This is a situation which has all the aspects of reality and necessity. And while the historical events came to a tragic end, with Agnes delivered to the executioner, to free Albrecht for the succession to the throne, there is no reason why Hebbel, without distorting the historical facts, could not have crowned the death of Agnes and the sadness of Albrecht with the glory of a shining example lighting the path to more humane thinking. As it is, he converts Albrecht to the acceptance of a 'Staatsräson' which in extreme cases demands and excuses such a sacrifice. Hebbel tries hard enough to bring Albrecht on his knees, mainly by frightening him with the certainty of unavoidable civil strife and devastation of a country which otherwise would enjoy peace. Even more, Hebbel makes Duke Ernst say that he is under no illusion as to the pragmatic value of such reasons of state; they are at best an expedient to wrest some sort of order from chaos, an agreement of temporary validity among the inhabitants of the earth, to guarantee a measure of peace and prosperity. What can be achieved by such a tradition, little as it may be, must not be jeopardized by the personal likes and dislikes of the rulers, for they are the ones who can 'das an sich Wertlose stempeln und ihm einen Wert beilegen'. Of all the relative values, that of orderly society has priority. Hebbel nowhere drops a hint that with the sacrifice of Agnes a torch was lit, as with the death of Antigone. The keynote of optimism, early in the play, has turned into resignation, and Hebbel no longer projects the forward thrust of dialectic process. The scepticism which he had long voiced in his diaries but muted in his creative work has finally invaded his drama. His heroic struggle to ward off, with the support given by classical form and thought, increasing misgivings about man's faculty to comprehend life as something meaningful, has come to an end.

One of the pivotal insights recorded in the diaries is that the new drama, 'if it comes into being, will differ from Shakespearean drama, which we shall have to surpass, by the fact that the dramatic dialect will have to reside not merely in the characters, but also in the idea itself, so that not only man's relationship to the idea, but the validity of the idea itself will be discussed.' This—said in 1843—is a clear anticipation of modern apprehension about the objective values of our ideas, and there are many such sceptical statements in the diaries. Against incipient nihilism Hebbel has to brace himself with some ethical imperative, as when in a letter to the philosopher and political writer Arnold Ruge, December 11, 1847, he says that we may have a right to feel resigned with regard to ourselves, but not with regard to mankind and its eternal rights and interests. The social obligation is, in other words, the one force that ought to keep us alive and optimistic—as it did most nineteenth-century writers— regardless of our private apprehensions. Hebbel's dream is of a time when the aims of art and those of society will coincide, linked

by the same desiderata for universal peace and happiness. Close as
he comes here to the main stream of nineteenth-century popular
literature, all this insight and effort of will cannot prevent him from
yielding to sceptical moods and from submitting to a merciless
intellectual dissection of life. He can in his diaries remind himself
that art is for the enjoyment of everybody, but his own production
was much more demanding. He is at times conscious of this fact and
complains that his own plays have too many entrails, and those of
his contemporaries too much skin, but he can do nothing to provide
them with both, in adequate proportion. He could well say that the
poet has to impart life to a reality which critical minds have, un-
fortunately, analysed to the point of dissolving, but he found it
impossible to control his own analytic bent. Early in his career he
strained himself to legitimate the existence of art at the side of
philosophy— art is realized philosophy, and without art philosophy
would have no point of reference and no means to check its own
conclusions. But in the course of time Hebbel came to learn that
systematic philosophy gave way to empirical and analytic thinking,
and that the latter held a powerful fascination for the artist as well.
He tried in vain to lift himself by his own boot-straps out of his
nihilism. His diaries betray an impressively honest desire to see to
the bottom of things, regardless of the fear that there was no hope
of finding solid ground again. There are few recent observations on
the questionable nature of the 'gedeutete Welt', the world as we
have naïvely interpreted it, which Hebbel has not already made, and
we can watch how the firm Hegelian structure, which had given
him his dialectic thesis of progressive movements, begins to collapse.
Not that he went on writing drama as if nothing had happened to
his once strong convictions; the fact that he lodged his conflicts in
the past and abstained from dramatizing contemporary dialectic
stirrings which were ushering in a better world indicates his uncertainty. He was, on the other hand, not ready to proclaim the
illusory nature of purposeful living, as Büchner had done. If his
often voiced opinion that the artist must be interested in the well-
being of society was no longer able to shore up a measure of optimism, his conscience as an artist helped him to retain his trust in the
implicit value of the creative act. Yet it is to his credit that he did
not make the next step—so often taken after Nietzsche—and content

himself with the satisfaction of aesthetic experience in a world devoid of all meaning. His heroes—and the author himself—live and die still yearning for absolute values, though they have no guarantee that such ideals exist. Hebbel operates in what Klaus Ziegler calls the 'Niemandsland zwischen Gläubigkeit und Glaubenslosigkeit: im Bereich der letzteren ist sein Drama noch nicht, und im Bereich der ersteren ist es nicht mehr zu Hause.'

He was as much as Nietzsche aware of the debilitating effect which passive intellectuality can have on our will to act. Long before Nietzsche he deplored the neglect of strict forms and the coming of an operatic age. His comments on the power of instinct and intuition over reason, his recognition that our concept of reality is predetermined and coloured by the mother tongue we speak, his many contributions to what later was to constitute depth psychology, his views of dreams as guides into and explorers of still unknown realities, all this is evidence of the deep shafts Hebbel had driven into areas beyond accepted concepts of reality.

There were others who found the surface of reality crumbling. Annette von Droste-Hülshoff (1797–1848) may not have been fully conscious of the enigmatic aspects of some of her works. The two collections of poems, in 1838 and 1844, oscillate both between surprising craftsmanship and dilettantism and between a conventional apprehension of reality and a penetratingly independent look at it. To reinforce the Catholic belief in which she had grown up, she wrote a cycle of religious poems, *Das geistliche Jahr* (1815), but with all her empathy into Christian mythology she could not silence her doubts and relieve an underlying melancholy. 'Not' and 'Sorge', the cues of modern existentialism, prevail over the vocabulary of solace and confidence, and instead of coming to rest in the grace of God she found herself questioning the comforts of religion. Immensely sensitive to all suffering, compassionate towards all living beings, and towards plants and animals as well, she conceived of a mythology in which the fall of man had dragged all nature into the abyss of misery; in addition to our own salvation we must strive for that of all other things created by God; we are burdened with a frighteningly difficult task from which there is only the temporary relief of an occasional abandonment to rare manifestations of unspoilt natural beauty. Trying to find refuge in traditional beliefs she had hit upon a new mystery, nature in need of redemption. Concomitantly, the habit of precise observation that made her style an anticipation of impressionism led her to probe deeper into reality; unable to stop at the poetic realism of most of her contemporaries she went on seeing things and seeing through them, to question customary views of reality. Many of her poems take us first through an array of surprisingly nuanced perceptions of sense objects, and end by making us afraid of the mystery behind them. It was only in her last years that she could lose herself, now and then, in rapturous wonderment at life's manifestations on land, on water or in the air, in order to keep the darker powers at bay.

The work that takes us more than any other into the depths of uncertainty and confuses our hopes for an intelligible world is *Die Judenbuche* (1842). Though small in size this novella stands out in nineteenth-century fiction, as if to make mock of all the cleverly devised plots, channelled into rational solutions. The sub-title *Ein Sittengemälde aus dem gebirgichten Westfalen* seems to set us on the trail of her folkloristic *Bilder aus Westfalen* (1842). But the narrator soon deviates from the path of realism, to bewilder us with all sorts of uncertainties. Has the hero of the story, Friedrich Mergel, first been an accessory to the murder of a forester and later become the murderer of a Jewish merchant? Or was this crime committed by some double of his who mysteriously turns up, from time to time, at his side? Which of the two—if two there are—is found hanging from the beech tree where the merchant was slain? These are strange questions to come from a text that is as lucid as any piece of realistic narration. Some readers will consider the circumstantial evidence good enough to convict Friedrich posthumously, while others suspect all hints thrown out in this direction as so many feints. When the murder of the Jew comes to light, one of his friends has the tree marked with an inscription in Hebrew: 'If you come near this place, you will suffer the fate you made me suffer.' Are we to take this as yet another lead? Trees are sacred and endowed with supernatural forces, and the beeches felled by the wood thieves Friedrich was associated with will sooner or later extract their retribution, even if Friedrich has to turn murderer first before becoming a suicide. A rationalist balks at such an explanation and will probably prefer a recently advanced view which is to the effect that Droste-Hülshoff simply wanted to impress the difficulty of sitting in judgment over others, since reality is much too complex to comply with our piece-meal insight. It is a conclusion at which the author seems to have arrived in many of her works, and which makes her an early defector from the straight path of realism and its identification with socio-political aims.

If it were not for the vortex of destruction into which men and women are being drawn in *Maler Nolten* (1832), we should hesitate to include Eduard Mörike (1804–75) among the writers who are difficult to explain in the context of nineteenth-century literature and who have to be seen as preparing us for the existential questions of a later period. For there is much in Mörike's world that seems to be naturally embedded in a homespun tradition. Steeped though he was, as a student of theology at the Tübinger Stift, in classical literature, he could not be drawn into aesthetic or philosophical discussions, and many of his poems seem to exemplify the finest flowerings of Swabian 'Biedermeier'—a most intimate evocation of a poetic and idyllic world left unruffled by social and political problems, and where any limitations, it would appear, are compensated by a vibrantly refreshing awareness of the things around us, nature, the hours of the day and the seasons of the year, by the sheer joy of being alive and of walking and talking, alone or with others. Mörike can muse in 'Der alte Turmhahn' over the old weathercock of Cleversulzbach, one of the several parishes where the poet served as pastor before retiring, at an early age, from clerical duties; the piece of scrap-iron, now lying in his study, will stir up a wealth of reminiscences and emotions, even amorous ones, but only to prompt the poet to formulate his message of the necessity of protecting our inner life against the outside world. The range of Mörike's 'Erlebnisdichtung'—never since Goethe so free from all dross—is relatively wide and includes nature and art as sources of experience.

But with *Maler Nolten* in the back of our mind we cannot fail to sense the precarious foundation of Mörike's tranquil world and to hear overtones of melancholy and fear. These occult and weird phenomena, which his Swabian countryman and friend Justinus Kerner (1786–1862) fondly used for spicing his fiction, were for Mörike much more of a threatening reality, and we suspect that he came at times close to being engulfed by the same psychological tensions which plagued and finally ruined another Swabian poet, Wilhelm Friedrich Waiblinger (1804–30).

With all the poise and control Mörike simulates in *Maler Nolten* he cannot prevent the darker forces from gaining the upper hand. While he still perorates on conventional problems such as the fusion of ancient with Christian art, a sort of Baudelairean voice becomes more and more audible, and the collapse of a hitherto secure cultural structure is recorded with both horror and fascination. In the year of Goethe's death Mörike's novel discloses a reality in which serious effort, excellent professional qualifications, and well-meant intentions are swept away by dark powers. There is no explanation for these, and the apparent double motivation— the revengeful hatred of a gipsy girl and the mental make-up of the principal characters—which in the opinion of many critics accounts for the final catastrophes, has no compelling force. The defeat of so much goodwill must be charged to the author, who brings his world crashing down, if not with a cynical delight then perhaps with the feeling that a horrible end is easier to bear than an unending horror.

It is as if Mörike, surviving this early collapse, had run—though at his own leisurely pace—for shelter into a life of few contacts with the outside world, but rich in inner values. As was said above, he did not engage in philosophical speculation and not even his intellectual friends like Kerner, Friedrich Theodor Vischer and David Friedrich Strauss could draw him into an exchange of ideas. If it was his conviction that the experience of beauty more than anything supports us in our will to live, he left it to Nietzsche to voice such a view, for himself he merely wanted to create such beauty in perfectly wrought poems. As for ideas and moral tenets, he needed none of the former and few of the latter. Some basic Stoic-Christian rules of conduct sufficed to give him his bearings. His predilection was for the golden mean between excess of joy and sorrow, not an inspiring message, but one that he had to practise if he wanted to preserve that tranquillity of mind which enabled him to remain attuned to the lastingly beautiful things in nature and art. Most of his poems are a perfect expression of this equilibrium between the poet and his surroundings. 'Um Mitternacht', 'Mein Fluss', 'Gesang zu zweien in der Nacht', 'Auf eine Christblume', 'Auf eine Lampe' have no equal in

German in their ability to draw man and nature or art into an enchanted circle of quiet communication, wonderment, serenity and love, with never a single component asserting itself too loudly. We can read these and other poems as perfect specimens in the tradition of Goethe, Storm, Keller, Carossa and the early Hesse and be all but oblivious of their origin in a difficult personality.

One of Mörike's last works, however, the novella *Mozart auf der Reise nach Prag* (1856), is a transparence of many hues, sombre and bright. This seemingly simple episode in Mozart's life turns, under the eyes of a sensitive reader, into a many-faceted jewel. The musician, travelling with his wife Konstanze to Prague, to conduct the first performance of his *Don Juan*, strays during a halt on his journey into the park of a castle. Seeing an orange-tree he holds one of its fruits in his hand, indulges in an Italian reminiscence of his youth, and inadvertently plucks the orange from its branch. The gardener who chances on the scene informs his masters of this act of pilfering, as he sees it—the tree is a sort of heirloom meant to be given as a present to the young woman whose betrothal is about to be celebrated. However, the incident merely helps to introduce Mozart and his wife as welcome guests to the castle. For a couple of days the worlds of refined society and of art become one in a symbiosis of rococo manners and interests, the itinerant composer is warmly received and the aristocrats thereby reveal a true inner calling to their high place in society. All this happens when the days of both are numbered—with Mozart showing symptoms of the illness to which he will succumb, and the carefree existence of the nobility threatened by the rumblings of revolution. These are at least the portents which we dimly perceive. The very fullness of these serene and happy hours seems to carry the seed of destruction in it; so much refined life can only be had at the price of death, or so we are made to feel. It is only a short step from this perfect musical consonance of the life and death themes to a theoretical exposition of them—but Mörike does not switch from the delicately sensuous instrumentation of the motifs and portents to explanatory prose. The problem expounds itself in the overtones of the narration, life and death rise as the two melodies that intertwine in a muted rhapsody on the union of art and life in the embrace of death.

Mörike's last years were increasingly marked by the anxiety that had informed his *Maler Nolten*. His misgivings extended to the value of art and creative work as well and it was only his unwillingness to perorate on *taedium vitae* that saved him from becoming the prophet of gloom and despair.

One of Mörike's close friends, Friedrich Theodor Vischer (1807–87) foreshadows another development that came to fruition in the twentieth century, the intellectual and essayistic novel. *Auch Einer* (1879), once widely read, though it has now fallen into disfavour as a narrative *tour de force*, deserves to be remembered for its aphoristic wisdom and as a cry in the wilderness—Vischer gallantly fought the nihilistic tendencies of his days, an aftermath, as he saw it, of romantic decadence which he wanted to overcome by passionate insistence on the reality of a higher sphere of values with power to engage us in purposeful aspirations. He did better in his satirical writings, notably in his *Faust*, to which reference was made in our introduction. If he did not become, as he might well have, the prototype of the *poeta doctus*, the intellectual writer of our times, he developed into a most discerning critic of contemporary literature and a philosopher who made lasting contributions to aesthetic theory. With Feuerbach he was instrumental in modifying Hegelian speculation by checking it against the facts of empirical investigation. Vischer represents a tradition, long lost now, in which the learned academic like himself or like the literary historian Hermann Hettner (1821–82) played the part of friend, consultant and adviser to many a creative writer.

Conrad Ferdinand Meyer (1825–96) is the last writer to be considered in the context of this chapter. He is, more evidently than any of the others, the poet in whose work the realism of nineteenth-century literature had to give way to new forms and content. The anti-realistic trend was in the air, around 1870, when with the rise of the new 'Kaiserreich' a wave of patriotic-heroic writing conjured up visions of monumental scope and socialistic and liberal thinking was relegated to the realm of bourgeois philistinism—'Übermensch' and Zarathustra are in the wings. Most of the pseudo-idealistic and pseudo-heroic writing of those days proved entirely ephemeral, the new poetic canons had to wait for men of real talent, and Meyer was one of them. It is interesting to see that he too was carried off his feet by the German victory of 1871, feeling the breeze of a more dynamic reality. But these and other vague elations had, in his case, to go through the filter of severely adhered-to aesthetic sensibilities.

Professor Henel sees Meyer as the initiator, in German literature, of a symbolism that later was to culminate in Rilke. With Meyer the epoch of 'Erlebnisdichtung', if it did not come to an end, had run into the competition of a different yet autonomous mode of lyrical creation.

Keller and Meyer were contemporaries and lived in the same city. In temperament and social background they stood wide apart. Even if he had wanted to, Meyer could not have written like Keller, by virtue of his artistic instincts. But it is well to remember that Meyer on occasions confessed to a feeling of envy for Keller's closeness to the people and his uncontested role of the spiritual mentor of their native city and country. Meyer experienced the secret longing of the esoteric artist and aloof patrician for the intimacies of ordinary life long before Thomas Mann embodied this conflict in Tonio Kröger, and his creative work, with all its formal exquisiteness, yearns for social contact and significance; he was never the *l'art pour l'art* poet we encounter among his symbolist successors.

Professor Henel has brilliantly shown how, in rewriting his poems, Meyer refashioned what was initially an autobiographical component—though often a rarefied aesthetic experience to begin with— into a highly symbolic form of expression. Frequently one and the same first impulse leads to proliferation in many directions, resulting in a number of poems, with subtle family traits to indicate their common origin. Such perfectly wrought poems as 'Zwei Segel', 'Der römische Brunnen', 'Säerspruch', 'Stapfen', not to mention many others, have all had a long lineage of predecessors and undergone a number of transformations before obtaining Meyer's stamp of approval.

It is more difficult to characterize Meyer's fiction in terms of innovation and departure from traditional narration. For his forms were slow in catching up with the changes in plot and motive. The style and composition of his only novel, *Jürg Jenatsch* (1876), a fairly early work, follow recognized standards of historical fiction, but the material—taken from the Thirty Years War, as it affected the Grisons—is handled in novel fashion; Meyer is less concerned with bringing the past to life than with underlining some essential characteristics of historical processes. Whether or not it was Bismarck who influenced him, he makes of Jenatsch the activist *par excellence*, a man who will commit every crime that his ideal political goal, the liberation of his native country, requires of him. Men of the honesty and humanity of the Duc de Rohan, the friend of Jenatsch and later betrayed by him, are on the other hand without influence on historical action. The great figures in history must be judged by a different code of ethics, or better still judged by their success. Meyer's obvious fondness for strong, ruthless men has been alternatively explained as an antidote to his own basic passivity or to the malaise of living in a small state which by its neutrality excluded itself from the scene of large-scale action. We need not indulge in such guess-work, because basically Meyer's interest is in the psychology of his characters, in the doubts and dissension rending the façade of strong-willed action. He anticipates the subtle psychological cases in the *fin de siècle* literature, when, in *Gustav Adolfs Page* (1882) he places a young girl disguised as a youth in the entourage of the king, a situation fraught with delicate problems, or when in *Das Leiden eines Knaben* (1883) he delves into the soul of a gifted but tender-minded boy who suffers at the hands of his elders and teachers.

However, men in exalted positions proved to be the most rewarding material for Meyer's psychological studies. In *Die Versuchung des Pescara* (1887) he makes of Pescara's temptation to betray the king by whom he has been deeply slighted a cat-and-mouse play in his own soul; with premonitions of his impending death Pescara gives free rein, imaginatively, to his plans for revenge, secure and at ease in his knowledge that nothing will come of it—he can have it both ways, Machiavellian and Christian. But it was in the story of Thomas Becket that Meyer found his most challenging human enigma. He did not, as he promised his publisher, solve the riddle of Becket's personality, but he composed a plot for *Der Heilige* (1879) by which the two conflicting halves in Becket could be rendered plausible and brought to a dramatic climax of interaction. We first meet Becket the humanist and learned man, who with his Moorish background and religious disinterestedness prefigures the man of enlightenment. He is happy to serve King Henry II as his chancellor, with no responsibility for the decisions that are to be made and no interest in them, except where his sense of justice and tolerance is hurt. To account for the abrupt change from friendship to hatred of the king Meyer invented the story of Becket's young daughter, who is seduced by the king and killed in an attempt to abduct her. Becket's chance for revenge comes when he is made Archbishop of Canterbury. He did not, we are given to understand, seek this office and even less the opportunity to avenge himself. As a matter of fact, he pleads with the king never to give him into the hands of a master who is stronger than the king himself. But now that God is his master he must fight the king in His name as the oppressor of the indigenous Saxons, though it is hardly possible that he does not, subconsciously, fuse personal and political motives in his quarrels with Henry II. He fights and humiliates the king both as an obedient servant of Christ and an outraged father, just as he attracts the wrath of the king for political reasons and because the king has a guilty conscience. It is a tangle of emotions that leads to the murder in the cathedral. Meyer continued unravelling the mysteries of human behaviour in *Die Hochzeit des Mönchs* (1884) and *Angela Borgia* (1891).

More and more Meyer began to mirror some of these human complexities in his very style of narration, first of all, as one would expect, by treating the art of story-telling itself as a problematic undertaking. Almost all of Meyer's stories make use of a framework. This allowed him to unload the responsibility of recording on to some narrator within the frame, or better still, to complement the viewpoint of the narrator, or narrators, by his own attitude or even comments. As a result, the reader becomes cognizant of the far from simple problem of describing events and feels invited to judge things from yet another angle, his own, and to modify the perspectives of the narrators. The story of *Der Heilige*, for instance, is brought to Zurich by a maker of crossbows; he had been in the service of King Henry and now relates his experience to a clergyman friend. This seems a strange medium to transmit events of such intricacy, even if the narrator, by a good deal of eavesdropping and by questioning those who were close to the principal actors has sharpened his own interest and his insight into the unfolding drama. Moreover, the learned recipient of his tale draws him out and adds his own comments, and there is, of course, always the author to help out and clarify issues. It is, in this connection, noteworthy to see how often

Meyer has recourse to eidetic expression, by assembling his characters into a revealing group-picture or by making objects of art,
statues and paintings, speak for him. With this and with a highly
selective vocabulary he moves in the direction of symbolism and a
less realistic art.

We have mentioned Meyer's longing for the intimate appeal
Keller exercised on his readers. One way in which he hoped to reach
the common man was that of the humorous story. But in the two
attempts he made, in *Der Schuss von der Kanzel* (1877) and *Plautus
im Nonnenkloster* (1882) we have to concede defeat; hard as he tries
to squeeze humour from some forcibly arranged situations, it is at
best the student of literature who will oblige with a wry smile,
merely to acknowledge the well-meant effort. The case is of general
significance. Humour is the prerogative of peasant and bourgeois
literature and of the Austrian scene. Socialistic writing, in the early
days placed under a heavy ideological strain, shows little humour,
acrimonious as its satirical bent may be. The intellectual writers,
those who are preoccupied with philosophical penetration or problems of form, seem to be impervious to humorous moods—or
they are in no need of the functions which humour performs in
nineteenth-century literature. These functions are best studied in the
writings of Keller, Raabe, Fontane and Reuter. In a world of conflict and disharmony, with no firm beliefs to provide for total
engagement, in a world where scepticism is almost a component of
our ideal strivings and where a measure of frustration is anticipated,
humour renders many services, as a comforter, or as a power that
lifts the heavy chain of our tensions. On a higher level humour
bridges the gap between expectation and only partial fulfilment, or
it helps to put things *sub specie aeternitatis*. 'Humour, the most inborn and brilliant achievement of the spirit,' as Hesse says, does not
relieve us of the problems which religion and philosophy will no
longer solve for us, but it does provide for a more relaxed attitude
to them. At the end of bourgeois realism, when cautious hopes for
social and political progress tapered into unqualified resignation, it
was humour that saved resignation from waxing into despair. But
humour can do still more, it can act as a humanizing force that
makes us less imperious in our intellectual demands, more willing
to listen patiently to what others have to say, even predisposing us

to kindness and generosity. There are no 'tierernste Gesichter' among the German realists of the nineteenth century; humour dissolves tensions and brings the most disparate phenomena into a spectrum of soft pastel hues. While value judgments are by no means suspended, the values are seen to run into each other and to plead for restrained judging.

By a strange form of dialectics the humour of the realists saved them from being bogged down in extreme realism, that is to say from studying their environment with the eyes of the specialist, the sociologist, historian or psychologist; behind realism there was the lurking danger of surrendering artistic autonomy to scientific investigation. Humour was able to transform the realities of the specialists back into a largely independent poetic experience of life, thus freeing the creative writer from the fetters of an excessive empiricism and regaining for him his own unique sphere of experience. 'Der Humor ist die einzige absolute Geburt des Lebens'— this was said by Hebbel, the intellectual writer who cast longing eyes on those who with the charisma of humour were privileged to evoke, over and above the ordinary world, an enchanted realm of serenity and freedom. Contemplation and religion had, in earlier times, helped man to a similar ecstasy, the word taken in its original meaning of getting outside the gravitational pull of common reality.

The subtlety of humour, as it appeared in realistic fiction, was largely beyond the range of the masses. To satisfy their needs the Germans had Wilhelm Busch (1832–1908). With the double gifts of a highly talented artist and dryly sarcastic, explosively laconic versifier he evoked peals of laughter from generations of readers. Busch's humour keeps us in a splendidly entertaining isolation from the world, but it is unable to exercise a humanizing charm. For the latter we have to go to Raimund and Nestroy, Fontane and Keller and to discover in Raabe's work the kind of humour which transforms reality into a serene other world without lacking the force to transform us into more human beings.

5   *Marxist and Socialist Literature*

George Steiner in *The Death of Tragedy* rightly assigns to Marxism the character of a modern mythology, the third one in western civilization, preceded by the mythology of the Greeks and by that of Christianity. Yet he seems to feel somewhat uneasy about Marxism in this illustrious company, since 'the Marxist world view came into being through political fiat rather than by the ripening of collective emotion', and because it was 'created at a specific time by a particular group of men, yet imposed upon the lives of millions'.

But if we say 'socialism' for 'Marxism', or include Marxism in the vast sphere of socialistic thought we come more nearly to a true mythology—an expanding force of ideas and visions which strike a sympathetic chord in countless men and women who share a desire for solidarity among all men, and for justice and freedom from want. United by their social hopes millions of people understand each other and respond to a common set of slogans and symbols. This is too obvious in the twentieth century to require comment. In the nineteenth century we witness, on the other hand, if not the origin of socialism—its beginnings date back to much earlier times; there is hardly a century after the rise of Christianity which did not witness some invigorating breeze of idealistic socialism—then at any rate a strong consolidation of socialistic aims. Literature was largely responsible for this.

If we look for professed Marxist literature in the nineteenth century—a literature informed by Marx and accepting his particular brand of socialism—the yield is small and provided by a few writers who at one time or other belonged to the entourage of Marx and Engels. If we think of socialism in its broader sense, we hear a steadily growing chorus of voices that plead for social ideas and their implementation. This is not surprising when we remember the social and political texture of the literature of Young Germany. The wonder is that socialist writing, with the impetus given by Young Germany, did not expand much faster and outgrow the other mythologies.

To start with Heinrich Heine (1797–1856) is to take the case which is least difficult, methodologically speaking. For whether we regard him as a romantic poet, or as the first great modern writer, the involvement in political thinking is always there. He grew out of romanticism by virtue of his compelling interest in society, and he became a modern stylist because of his social convictions. This is the way his admirers saw Heine, and though the histories of literature all too often prefer to record the voices of those who disparaged his eminence, all those who, in the words of Gottfried Keller, stood 'on the green side of life' revered him as their patron saint. His work in form and content is marked by a sharp turn away from outworn modes of thought and feeling to an anxious concern with social and political realities.

In 1844 Marx, in his *Deutsch-Französische Jahrbücher*, published Heine's satirical 'Lobgesänge auf König Ludwig'. As a token of gratitude Heine sent him the proofs of his verse epic *Deutschland: ein Wintermärchen*, and Marx cannot have failed to experience what the poet hoped he would, 'some fun'. Marx, and Marxism for that matter, have not often been presented with a greater literary gift, supreme art and delectable art, a mordant exposure of the reactionary Germany Heine encountered when, in 1843, he revisited his home country. Together with *Atta Troll* (1843), the *Wintermärchen* stands out as his most sustained effort at political satire. But this was only a beginning, with the best political poems yet to come. With 'Die schlesischen Weber', 'Die Wanderratten', 'Das Sklavenschiff', to mention only a few, Heine proved the possibility of great social and political lyrics, a proof which so many well-meaning rhymesters of the turbulent Forties failed to establish. But Heine never contented himself with plucking the chords of irreverence and radical attack. His *Neue Gedichte* of 1844, republished and augmented in 1852, his *Romanzero* (1851) and the poems he wrote from then on encompass a wide variety of human experience. Bedridden for the last eight years of his life, he experienced, on his 'Matratzengruft', all the horrors of the human predicament, yet he remained unbroken in his intellectual capacities and his inner resources, still running the vaudeville show that Barker Fairley has brought to our attention, and calling on many characters to perform for us and delight us with songs within song, dance and theatricals. But Heine also continues, with greater penetration than ever, to probe the depth of humanity. Mr. Prawer holds that Heine's vitality was bound to make him run over the whole keyboard of experience, from the spiritual to the sensuous. He did so even in his years of abject suffering; hardly able to hold his pen, he writes not mainly, as one would expect, of his personal agony, but keeps himself tuned as the medium through which life as such, or his own life in its entirety, becomes resonant. *Gedichte 1853 und 1854*, and later poems, contain notes of unmitigated misery, but also some of the most militant social verse, such as 'Erinnerung an Hammonia'. And where the tone is that of bitterness and sweetness together, as in 'Mein Tag war heiter', the bitter component is not supplied by his illness, but by the realization of death, and the balance is tipped on the side of acceptance and *joie de vivre*, lifting the last lines to a subdued paean on life. The feat is remarkable in the light of present-day lamentations of the existentialists. Heine rises from the abyss of real suffering, while so many modern poets jump into the pit of despair for no other reason than a fashionable 'Angst'. To attribute Heine's courageous attitude to nothing but 'Galgenhumor' is to underestimate the source of strength. He could speak of the sweetness of life in the face of the most painful personal suffering because he had wrested from life achievements of lasting satisfaction, works of art, which by their beauty and their humour would continue to delight; and—perhaps the most coveted memory—he knew that he had stood in the vanguard of the fight for justice and freedom. He saw himself as the torch-bearer of socialism:

> Ein Posten ist vakant! Die Wunden klaffen—
> Der eine fällt, die andern rücken nach—
> Doch fall' ich unbesiegt, und meine Waffen
> Sind nicht gebrochen—nur mein Herze brach.

The significance of this, Heine's victory over despair by means of a clear conscience, has yet to be grasped by his readers. It was the sense of real service to our fellow-men which lent him such power of resistance to the blows of fate.

Heine resumed the impulses of the Enlightenment and brought the qualities of reason to his life and work. This intellectual vein is obvious enough in his fiction and essays. *Die romantische Schule*

C

(1836), and even more *Zur Geschichte der Religion und Philosophie in Deutschland* (1834), scoff at the mystic or myopic tradition in German self-portrayal. Though the astringency of his prose was powerless to save German philosophical and scientific writing from the bane of turgidity, the flashes of his lucidity sufficed to set standards for creative writers; the admiration which Hebbel, Keller, Raabe, Storm, Fontane and others had for Heine was born of gratitude for what they had learned from him. The fact that nineteenth-century fiction remained, by and large, comprehensible for people of normal intelligence owes much to Heine's style.

The wonder of it all is that he did or could have done the same for poetic diction. His verse can be as lyrical as any, yet the emotions are never without a clear relation to a logocentric base. Conversely, he can roam through distant times and places, observe and describe the nuances of all of them and still make the details serve his intellectual and emotional intents. With all their length, poems like 'Vitzliputzli' or 'Rhampsenit' never break apart in their basic mood; they grow in the first case into a resounding crescendo of man's brutality, and in the latter dissolve into a serene acceptance of life's strange ways. His 'Hebräische Melodien' take us into a cultural sphere which was at that time largely unknown to German readers, and Heine treats us to as much factual knowledge as lyrical apprehension of a foreign world. The exploratory powers of his style show to best advantage in his excursions into Parisian life, but again the novelty of the subject is not presented for its own sake, but used to proclaim the delight of erotic experience and to make intelligible its manifestations on the lower levels of society. Heine practises no discrimination between high and low, respected and despised. For earth, he said when commenting on a picture by Leopold Robert, is heaven, and mankind is sacred, imbued with a divine spirit. That no one should be deprived of his share in this heavenly inheritance was ingrained in Heine's thought and formed the basic motivation of his later writing. Some writers of the Young Germany group may have hit upon elements of a similarly modern style and perhaps have been more explicit in their political ideas. What they lacked was his specifically poetic gift, his genius for turning the social battle into a delightful aesthetic experience without in any way weakening our zest to participate in the struggle for the under-privileged—part of a larger fight for the life of reason.

Heine's influence on progressive-minded European writers is a matter of record. Ironically enough, the one man who was more nearly than any other writer his successor had long fallen into a neglect from which he is only now being retrieved. Georg Weerth (1822–56) held leading positions in the inner circle of European socialists. In 1848 and 1849 he served as literary editor of the *Neue rheinische Zeitung*, the short-lived paper with which Marx hoped to win support for socialism. By trade a clerk and book-keeper, Weerth had gained valuable insight into business practices which, gifted satirist that he was, he turned to good litearry use. His sojourns in England did much to help him understand industrial society and to strengthen his misgivings about it. His articles on life in England, published between 1843 and 1848, reveal him to be a sympathetic student of social conditions, touched by the plight of the workers and looking for remedies, but fair enough to come to his conclusions after consulting an impressive list of historical and statistical material. These essays are now published as *Skizzen aus dem sozialen und politischen Leben der Briten*, and with a number of reports on his socialistic and communistic activities they secure Weerth an honourable place in the history of early socialism. But Weerth's ambition went further than that and bade him serve the great cause as a creative writer. His poems attest his satirical talents, though these are less incisive than Heine's, probably because Weerth had more of that humour which can envisage the ultimate reconciliation of conflicting forces and condone the lack of repentance in some bourgeois characters. The fragment of a novel written around 1846 was meant to show the impact of a young German worker, who during his stay in England had turned chartist and socialist, on the political backwardness of his native land. But much as the hero tries to 'conjure up a better and more beautiful time' for the benefit of the proletarians, Weerth's intention does not integrate with the requirements of fiction, and the progress of the work was hampered and finally arrested by an obvious split between editorials put in the mouth of the young socialist and the temptation to have a satirical field day with the enemy camp of bourgeois and noblemen. Weerth gave his best where he made satire the exclusive perspective for exposing the rotten state of affairs. *Leben und Taten des berühmten Ritters Schnapphahnski* was a great success when it appeared in the *Neue rheinische Zeitung* and Heine's publisher Campe brought the novel out in book form. However, by that time the censors had been alerted; they sentenced the author to a prison term of three months, which he served at Cologne. It was evident, without Weerth's explicit admission, that he strove to continue in the spirit of Heine's *Atta Troll* and, we might add, of *Aus den Memoiren des Herren von Schnabelewopski*, with the purpose of lashing the brutality, mendacity and criminality of one Fürst Lichnowski, a shady nobleman and unworthy member of the Prussian Diet. While we no longer draw comparisons with Cervantes and Rabelais, we can understand that Heine was interested in his disciple and asked Marx to introduce him to Weerth. The untimely death of the latter nipped in the bud one of the early hopes for a great socialist writer, and it was not until Heinrich Mann's *Der Untertan* (1918) appeared that political satire on the grand scale aligned itself again with progressive politics.

The most resounding effect on early socialism issued, of course, from the *Communist Manifesto* of 1848, an effect which was due in no small measure to the literary quality of its prose, working on and softening our emotions and at the same time driving our thoughts with dramatic compulsion to seemingly incontestable conclusions. Even if one can resist the argumentation of the manifesto, one is hardly able to shake off the spell of its literary appeal. This was an astounding manifestation of the power of the word, helped, of course, by a combination of favourable circumstances. The plight of the proletarians had been described with greater compassion before, and their rights had been more cogently argued and defended. But the hour was on the side of Marx, as it had not been on the side of Büchner or of Wilhelm Weitling (1808–71), the sincerely enthusiastic prophet of a religious socialism, or on the side of Bettina von Arnim (1785–1859). Bettina's social ideas are more definitely in competition with Marx than any other body of early socialistic thought. *Dies Buch gehört dem König* (1843) is by far the boldest declaration of human rights and the most insistent attack on the apathy of the upper classes that had been delivered in the first half of the 19th century. She is the first one to ask for total humanism, for a sympathy that extends to all human beings, regardless of their short-comings, and the criminal is most emphatically singled out as the test of our love and understanding. Bettina's emotions and the conclusions she draws from them for the implementation of un-reserved kindness and justice issue from her cosmology; God wants a happy world, and he leaves it to us to complete his creation. To work for the well-being of mankind is our built-in destiny, as it is also our most blissful experience. From her spiritual background of romantic philosophies of identity Bettina evolves that kind of absolute socialism which accords with the great tradition of classi-cal and romantic 'Humanität'. Her protest against the abuse of power and privilege and her demand for absolute humanity in the conduct of all public affairs gives the lie to the lack of interest in progressive social efforts so often alleged against German romantics. Bettina, Jean Paul in his political writings, and the life and works of Ludwig Uhland (1787–1862) bring German romanticism more closely in line with its English counterpart—a continuation of social visions and demands after the betrayal of these aspirations by the French revolution.

Of the host of minor poets kindling the revolutionary fire before 1848 Ferdinand Freiligrath (1810–76) was the most talented. His lyrical fanfares in *Ein Glaubensbekenntnis* (1844) and *Ça ira* (1846) made him the target of suspicion and prosecution, forcing him to seek refuge in Brussels, Switzerland and London, where he joined the group of socialists around Marx. However, he mellowed under the influence of age and disappointment, and when in 1868 he was allowed to return to Germany he arrived just in time to become the bard of the new Reich that was in process of forming, and to blow the patriotic trumpet during the Franco-Prussian War. Hoffmann von Fallersleben (1789–1874), on the other hand, had no thought of promoting the cause of nationalism when in 1841 he wrote what was to become the German national anthem, 'Deutschland, Deutsch-land über alles'. For he was a staunch democrat with an engagingly poetic mind. Georg Herwegh (1817–75) deserves to be remembered by his work and life-long devotion to socialism rather than by the unfortunate episode of 1848, when he headed an auxiliary corps he had collected among German exiles in France, to join the republican rebels in Baden, only to run for shelter into Switzerland after the collapse of the upheaval. In 1841 he electrified the Germans by his radical message in *Gedichte eines Lebendigen*, the best introduction to the staff of the paper Marx published in Cologne. Like his master he had to go into exile, from which he returned in 1866; undaunted in his courage and convictions he joined the ranks of class-conscious left-wing socialists, lending his poetic gifts to their fight for human rights and opposition to Prussian militarism.

Socialism, the attempt to secure greater freedom for the working population and a more equal distribution of material goods, is not, of course, confined to ideologists. Both causes have received much succour from all sorts of sympathizers. In bourgeois literature we find touching evidence of understanding for and compassion with the underprivileged, and many instances of sincere efforts to remedy the situation. The same is true of regional or peasant literature, or for the literature of Austria. Now and then concern with oppression in any form takes an author outside the range to which we might incline to relegate him. Nikolaus Lenau (1802–50)—his full name was Nikolaus Franz Nimbsch, Edler von Strehlenau—was born and brought up in Austria. His originality as a lyrical poet has never been contested; some of his poems, well formed and even better felt, did much to bring passion back into German lyrics. The heritage of Goethe, Heine and Byron continued in him with a highly independent response to life—the traditional 'Sänger' seemed to have been reborn as a kind of wild Hungarian fiddler, a near-genius, with streams of melodies flowing from his instrument, now frighteningly temperamental, now darkly melancholy, foreshadowing the madness in which Lenau's restless existence came to an end. But he was also endowed with a great gift for critical perception and inspired by a burning desire to serve mankind. German romanticism, as he saw it, had left no social and political guidelines—Bettina's manifesto had not yet been published—and he found his own country lamentably lacking in progressive drives; therefore he felt it incumbent on him to make literature an aid towards civilization and humanization. In 1832 he left Austria, saddened and angered by the lethargy of the Metternich regime, and hoping to find scope for his idealistic plans in North America. He came back the following year, with a trail of disappointments behind him. But this was not to discourage him; a better acquaintance with Hegel confirmed him in his social and political fervour. He started writing a lyrical epic on the Hussites, but saw his ideal intention blocked by the facts of history, the defeat of the Bohemian freedom-fighters; all he could do was to put in the mouth of dying Ziska an exhortation to renewed efforts. In the religious wars of the Albigenses he found more nearly what he wanted, if not the winning of complete victory then at least the most heroic struggle against papal oppression and obscurantism. *Die Albigenser* (1842), his 'boldest and grandest work', as Lenau called it, affects us to this very day with the spirit of rebellion against injustice and arrogance. State and Church, not to be deceived by the enduring beauty of so many parts of the work, were quick in relating Lenau's radicalism to the disease that was to destroy him. In a posthumously published verse epic, *Don Juan*, the poet makes the third demand in the triad of nineteenth century liberalism his own—the release from sexual taboos.

For a while, and with the evidence of his novel *Problematische Naturen* (1861), it looked as if Friedrich Spielhagen (1829–1911) was to take over from Lenau and other radicals, sending as he does all men of intelligence and goodwill, proletarians, intellectuals and aristocrats, to the barricades of social insurrection. But he broke off his political expedition—disappointed, so we are told, by the leaders of the socialistic movement, Engels and Lassalle, and spent long years on uncommitted fiction and verse, helped or hindered by an almost too conscious command of forms and techniques. His disquisitions in *Beiträge zur Theorie und Technik des Romans* (1882), mainly a plea for objectivity in fiction, mark the watershed between the old-type narrator pretending to be omniscient and the modern writer who feels less confident in the assembling of data and calls in additional narrators to assist him and provide for more than one perspective.

The deep human interest which the naturalists took in the lower depths of life and their contribution to socialistic thinking—often an emotional rather than a sociological approach—a preparation for ideas and action through stirring compassion—are dealt with at the beginning of the modern era in German literature in Professor Hatfield's volume.

In now turning to the other three mythologies—sustained by peasant and bourgeois writing and by the literature of Austria—we fully realize the questionability of such a nomenclature. We could, of course, bring the literature of the peasantry more in terminological accord with Austrian literature by calling it Swiss literature. But apart from the fact that this term is much too limited for the phenomenon we have in mind, we would still find it impossible to provide for the third group, bourgeois literature, a comparable regional or national definition. Again, while 'bourgeois' and 'peasant' are *in pari materia*, the Austrian field cannot possibly be reclassified by any such sociological term. We are faced with a theoretical inconsistency which disappears in the practice of literary history. If the three adjectives cannot be brought on the level of comparability, the nouns, literature in every case, can.

6   *Peasant Literature*

We referred to Immermann's *Oberhof* as an insertion in *Münchhausen* that soon became an independent piece of fiction—if not the first 'Bauerngeschichte' then one of seminal importance. The interest it aroused and the imitations it prompted reflect an obvious need to close a gap in German literature. The countryside and the people who tilled the fields had hardly been raised to literary awareness before that time. Classical writers with their bias for reduction to typical and general traits were oblivious of their existence—a growing realism could be expected to take cognizance of it and was in a better position to augment the inventory of the human scene. A more intensive concern with the social and political betterment of the masses went hand in hand with this interest.

Immermann's *Oberhof*, though not lacking in events and excitement, suffers slightly from what was to become the bane of peasant literature written by outsiders—turning the countryside into an exhibition of fokloristic items, or into a stage where old customs can be seen in action. The true spokesmen for the rural population, the real representatives of its realities and aspirations, do not resort to such dressing up in costume. It was fortunate that the re-emergence of peasant literature was taken in hand by two men who in their different ways wrote with a sense of mission—to leaven life in the rural districts and small towns with cultural and spiritual values, not so much to raise it to urban standards as to encourage it to find its own level and develop its own indigenous culture.

Johann Peter Hebel (1760–1826) serves as an early warning not to treat literature dealing with country people as something primitive, naïve and inferior, but on the contrary to recognize its many dimensions. Modern critics, emboldened by Kafka's affection for Hebel's narratives, think nothing of linking Hebel with modern existentialists and attributing to him some of the complexities of contemporary thinking. Goethe, on the other hand, spoke fondly of the author who made Alemannic German pliable for the finest poetic expression. Both these judgements point to a rare combination of naturalness with consciousness, of simplicity with sophistication. Hebel, in order to know simple people so well and to make them so quick with life in his poems and stories, must, we assume, have been one of them, but his formal perfection and even more his wise reflection and counselling make us at once recall that he also belonged to the educated part of mankind, as a professor of dogmatic theology and of Hebrew at the Karlsruhe 'Gymnasium', as a prelate and ex-officio member of the Baden Diet, and as a man who was at home in the works of Homer, Theocritus, Catullus, Virgil and Horace. More significantly, he regarded himself as a descendant of the Enlightenment, as a disciple of German classicism and its 'Humanität' and therefore obliged to raise his voice in the name of freedom and social sympathy. The surprise is that as a creative writer he does not have to exclude any of these gifts and inclinations. He can write poems on porridge—'Das Habermus'—on the folk-lore of New Year's Eve—'Der Geist in der Neujahrsnacht'— on the cry of the night-watchman—'Der Nachtwächter'—so close to the texture of these experiences that children delight in reading them, yet also with such clarity and courage of thought and such artistic refinement that adults find him a source of aesthetic joy and perennial wisdom. All this may explain why to this very day Alemannic people are in the habit of committing Hebel poems to memory in order to carry with them some of the finest treasures for mind and heart.

It is the same with his narratives. We can read most of them as 'Kalender' stories, enjoy them and think nostalgically of the days when such plain literary fare was the only reading material farmers and townspeople would turn to, apart from the Bible. But we will soon begin to speculate on how it happens that these stories, seemingly belonging to an archaic oral tradition, on closer reading reveal structures of many levels, to confuse and enchant us with a variety of facets, displaying before us a miniature world and inviting us to serious contemplation and penetration. Anecdotal material taken from everyday life, criminal cases, adventures from near and far, episodes involving historical characters or local men and women, thieves, and saints, Hebel fashions them in threefold perfection— crisp and clear reporting, serenely applied lesson and translucent humanity. He finds examples of broadmindedness and reason in all walks of life. If Napoleon, General Suvorov, or Mohammed, happens to provide a good story he never pollutes it with some injection of arrogant nationalism. His voice is never raised in partiality to high station in life, much as he likes to discover nobility—but it has to be nobility of mind. Wide as the range of themes and the geographical and chronological distribution is, his style—only another term for his mind—makes them serve to illustrate his scale of values and to underscore man's obligation to ideal aims. These are among the qualities that make his best known collection of prose, *Schatzkästlein des rheinländischen Hausfreundes* (1811), the treasure-chest mentioned in the title.

If, as we indicated, modern readers detect in Hebel's stories like *Kannitverstan* and particularly in *Unverhofftes Wiedersehen* a transition from a rational apperception of life to an involvement in the mysteries of being, a reality which tends to transform itself into an allegory or parable of unfathomable existence, this does not invalidate Hebel's basically rational philosophy; it merely confirms the wide confines of his sensibilities. We can recognize the bridge from him to Kafka, but it is a bridge over which we should have liked Kafka to come back to Hebel, to his serenity and his faith in mankind in spite of his contacts with the dark side of life. The aura of the mysterious at the edge of Hebel's reality is a natural phenomenon, evidence of his awareness of transcendence, not a trick to pull off alienation or frighten us into anxiety.

The foundation of Hebel's world is soundly real and tractable by human effort and intelligence, ready to absorb our goodwill and wisdom, eager to repay us with the gifts of life. Robert Minder in his essay 'Johann Peter Hebel und die französische Heimatliteratur' draws La Fontaine close to Hebel. Both received strength from a classical education, both hoped to make this heritage, on their own terms, available to common people, without loss of spiritual substance. Jeremias Gotthelf (1797–1854) joined them in this endeavour, but with greater concentration on the needs of his peasant environment.

At the age of 37 Albert Bitzius, a Protestant minister in the small peasant community of Lützelflüh, in the canton of Berne, found that he had some time on his hands and decided to try writing a book. After attempting a local chronicle he started a novel, which appeared in 1837 as *Der Bauernspiegel* under the pen-name of Jeremias Gotthelf, the name that was to displace his legitimate one. While remaining a conscientious pastor, an actively engaged inspector of schools and the co-founder and supervisor of an orphanage, Gotthelf managed to continue his literary career and to become one of the major novelists in German. The Swiss lineage is a strong determinant in his work and accounts for the spiritual imprint of a robust Christian humanism hewing close to practical application and keeping out of the clouds of mysticism or the maze of theological dogma. His immediate predecessor is Johann Heinrich Pestalozzi (1746–1827), the outstanding educationist and tireless humanitarian, rather than the well-meaning but sentimental writer and theologian Johann Caspar Lavater (1741–1801). Gotthelf succeeded in continuing his theological and social work in his creative writing; there was no need for him to wrestle like Tolstoy with the pangs of conscience and to wonder whether by spending long hours at his writing desk he was not neglecting a more direct obligation to suffering mankind. We have undisguised teaching and preaching in his novels, and some of it had its origin in an overt desire to combat abuses—alcoholism, for instance, or the medical quacks. But almost without exception his creative furore was powerful and resourceful enough to melt didactic elements into artistic form.

The basis for Gotthelf's missionary sense has been described as a fervent desire to preach and promote the sanctification of life. Pico della Mirandola's concept of human dignity, or of the possibility of obtaining such dignity, lies at the root of Gotthelf's thinking. As others before him, he likens man to a tree with roots in the soil and a crown growing heavenward. We are destined and equipped for a higher than material life, and with the proper kind of upbringing by our parents or some other mentor human beings can, with all their earthiness and despite the tributes exacted from them by a sensuous nature, attain to the level of rational and beneficent life. Gotthelf has time and again retraced in his fiction the paths of men and women who were at one point or other awakened and inspired to the reality of true humaneness and who manage to give a good account of themselves; human depravity resulting from a neglected call to serious striving assumes, on the other hand, frightening forms in his works.

But the point to make is this: Gotthelf, if he writes mainly of the peasants he knew so well, does not address himself to peasant readers only, but to all those who still live or yearn to live in a world of ascertained spiritual values. For the demonstration of such a world he preferred the hard-core reality of the countryside. The literature that concerned itself during the nineteenth century with these realities of rural existence did not always rise above a documentary regional form of writing. In the best instances, however, it achieved the projection of a self-contained world, rich in detail, teeming with human conflict, yet also unified by common beliefs. This world was smaller than the epic worlds of Homer and Dante— though Gotthelf and Fritz Reuter have often invited comparison with a Homeric world. The question was whether this peasant sphere—approximating to a mythology—would remain an enclave in the wider area of German civilization and gradually be reduced to the confines of an idyll, by-passed by the highways of modern developments, or whether it could expand—not, of course, by increasing the arable surface of a country, but by converting the workers and the middle classes to its own fundamental tenets. The answer to this was given by the intensified urbanization and industrialization of Germany, and by the fact that, socially and politically speaking, it was bourgeois thinkers and the workers, and not the farmers, who determined the patterns of change and progress.

The defeat, or at any rate the relegation to the minor role of a leavening force, which peasant literature suffered shows best in the language it tried to speak, a new idiom replenished by idiomatic expressions and dialect elements, freed from Greek and Latin domination, rediscovering its own Germanic foundation. Reuter wrote almost all his works in the Mecklenburg version of Low German, and while this gave him easy access to some thirty millions of Germans, from Hamburg to Königsberg, he was unable to induce the schools, churches and law courts to make 'Plattdeutsch' their official language, a prerequisite to the strengthening of Low German. Reuter's work remains confined, outside of North Germany, to those who are willing to make the linguistic effort. Even so, he had the advantage of a large segment of Germans who knew his language. Many other dialect writers had to content themselves with a much smaller group of linguistic intimates. Ludwig Thoma (1867–

1921), the Bavarian expounder of peasant literature, was wise enough to use dialect only sparingly and to cultivate a High German that stayed as racy as was possible in a literary environment imperilled by artistic sophistication and journalistic sloppiness. But there can be no talk of Thoma's having entertained the thought of making the peasant world linguistically as self-supporting as it was culturally.

Gotthelf, on the other hand, came close to giving his world a language of its own, though perhaps inadvertently. An early reader like Jacob Grimm, in his preface to the *Deutsches Wörterbuch*, spoke admiringly of the vividness of Gotthelf's style, and the sensuousness of his language has long become a household word in Gotthelf criticism. He can be vigorous to a fault, and the eruption of his language—always colourful and concrete—into metaphors and similes is apt to be both a delight and a strain. Yet it has always been felt that Gotthelf's writing, rather than betraying a naïve, self-taught talent, taps some hidden sources of Germanic communication; the gushing forth of a refreshing idiom recalled Luther's language and suggested the rebirth of a truly indigenous German, to replace a 'Lutherdeutsch' drained of its former vigour by Greek and Latin scholars. The Alemannic South seemed with Gotthelf to repeat what Luther's Bible translation had once achieved for the North. The German that Gotthelf wrote, 'Schweizerdeutsch', not 'Schwyzer-dütsch', promised to bring relief from outworn speech-patterns and to give the Germans a chance to express themselves again with simplicity and clarity. If the opportunity actually existed of invading Germany from the Alemannic periphery and restoring German to a more autonomous character, it was not exploited with any degree of persistence. Gotthelf never thought of such a conquest and more and more disqualified himself for it by failing to trim what looked like a new style of all harshly regional admixtures. There are other reasons why 'Schweizerdeutsch', a German growing out of a peasant mythology, out of a more elemental world, did not acquire enough momentum to penetrate nineteenth century German civilization. If 'Lutherdeutsch' spread on the waves of reformatory zeal and popular interest in the Bible, Gotthelf's novels, though widely read in Germany as well as in Switzerland, did not bring the message which masses of people were craving for. His works were for many simply a welcome supply of entertaining material, an excursion into a quaint archaic world, or a shock to those who knew the peasant only from Gessner's mid-eighteenth-century *Idyllen*. Gotthelf was, especially for urban readers, more a literary than a spiritual experience; he could treat them to a mirage of an archaic epic world, but not attract them to a kingdom to come. One final consideration comes to mind in this context. What German civilization needed, in the nineteenth century, was not a reformation of its literary language, but the extension of existing modes of expression and understanding into the widening areas of science, and industrial and technological developments. It is possible that the Germans, steeped in a literary culture, were looking in the wrong direction and expected salvation to come from sources which at most could supply good literature, decent craftsmanship and fine entertainment. They were hoping for some spiritual manna when what was needed was a better understanding of social and political realities. Small wonder that they were duped, first by the chiaroscuro tricks used by Wagner, and then by the stylistic and intellectual clowning of Nietzsche's *Zarathustra*.

Was Gotthelf primitive enough to believe that his world amounted to more than a convenient working hypothesis, a creation of his imagination for the untrammelled release of his narrative genius? We have four volumes of his sermons to show how readily the words came to him that his parishioners understood and how well he could give the impression of believing what they were supposed to believe as good Christians. Cutting out dogmatic quibbles as he did and using Christian terms as the language of a universal humanism and as an illustration of man's inborn desire for spiritual transformation, he need not, even as a pastor, feel ill at ease. As a narrator he gives the impression of being exuberantly happy in his peasant world. Here there was scope for him to daub colour on a vast canvas of realities, to discern the nuances of characterization for an astonishing assortment of men, women, and children, some almost saints and others worse than devils. The peasant scene more easily than any other milieu could be turned into the battlefield between good and evil, between ill will and serious effort. Farmers live largely by the grace of God and the weather he provides, a hailstorm can ruin the labour of months and release a flood of curses; a deep-felt gratitude, if all goes well, may quickly alternate with the urge to quarrel with fate; the play of human reactions, over the whole keyboard of emotions, proceeds uninterrupted. This challenge to the narrator was equalled by that to the spiritual adviser, the wrathful prophet, the kind comforter. Gotthelf reigned in this world as a kind of 'Statthalter Gottes', a minister with prerogatives far greater than those granted by the church. No need for him to search for plots and thrilling events, or for motifs and philosophical padding; he was spared the indecision between one genre and another, the narrative form was as adequate as it was genuine to him.

Gotthelf's first novel *Der Bauernspiegel* attests at once this happy correspondence between author and milieu. Using the form of autobiography he starts powerfully: 'I was born in the year which did not have its beginnings in the Christian calendar, in a community called Stupidity'. There is thus every reason for Gotthelf to set the process of christianization in motion. The obstacles are as formidable as they appear to be real. Jeremias reports on a wretched youth with parents whose prosperity and spiritual growth were stunted by ill luck and the absence of intelligence and initiative. As an orphan boy he is put on the auction-block and turned over to the highest bidder, to the 'buyers and exploiters of cheap child labour', and his first service is with irresponsible masters. But if there is misery and cruelty, there is also kindness and serious concern for the hapless child; a prosperous farmer who is a true Christian and feels responsible to God for the training of a neglected fellow-being is no unusual phenomenon in Gotthelf's world. More often—as in the *Bauernspiegel*—it is the love of a woman that stirs the best qualities in man. Though Jeremias loses his girl through death in childbed, the memory of her angelic disposition and devotion to him never fades and prepares the soil in which the seed of his own humanity will take root. In the end, after some years in the service of the French army, Jeremias returns, well enough provided to be in a position to lead the ideal life the author is able to envisage for him. He will settle down in a small community and give freely of his time as counsellor to people with problems, instructing their children and available with his experience and wisdom. Believing with Pestalozzi that a measure of education and training is indispensable for establishing self-respect and independence in men and women,

Gotthelf made his second novel, *Leiden und Freuden eines Schulmeisters* (1838–39), a means for investigating and castigating educational practices or their deficiences. Precise as the theme he set himself is, its elaboration and the conclusions he arrives at take us through a vast expanse of life—a reassuring indication that the didactic purpose can activate rather than constrict Gotthelf's imagination and his enjoyment of leisurely, richly anecdotal narration. *Uli der Knecht* (1841) and its sequel *Uli der Pächter* (1847) show, as the titles indicate, the advancement of a hard-working fellow to a position of relative comfort. Temptations of all kinds, worst of all those from wealth and selfishness, delay the maturing of insight and patience, and as in almost every work of Gotthelf we are made to feel that existence requires constant application to spiritual aims, if it is not to end with the remorseful realization of social uselessness, a form of mental punishment which is severe enough not to require any additional sentence—least of all that of eternal damnation. A more specific problem is treated in *Geld und Geist* (1843–44). The story concerns a rich, closely-knit family; the husband, through inexperience and good nature, loses a considerable sum of money, and his wife, now sulking and quarrelling, undermines all peace and happiness. Her refusal, for the first time since they were married, to join her husband in the customary evening prayer makes the rift seemingly irreparable. The same prayer, after a trying time of altercation, brooding and isolation, ushers in a new life of harmony. Wealth—this is one of the lessons driven home with drastic immediacy—is a blessing only where kindness and piety, friendliness and humility, prevail. Christian sermons, church bells and, as we indicated, prayers are powerful agents in restoring these people to their former bliss, yet such religious observances are effective only where there is some basic intelligence and mutual consideration to draw on. Gotthelf is not writing as a sectarian pastor, but as one who knows what the peasant community, and all other communities, for that matter, need in order to strive for peace and harmony: the strength of love which overcomes temporary aversions. In *Geld und Geist* as in many other stories it is the wife of the farmer who suffers most from her own short-comings and those of others and who takes the first remedial step to initiate the process of sanctification with renewed vigour. The conflict between material and spiritual treasures is fought out with subtle psychological arguments—the farmers are in this respect as sensitive and complex as any exponents of the soul's trials and tribulations in classical literature. *Die Käserei in der Vehfreude* (1850) is a contrast and counterpart, by virtue of its extroversion, involving the effort of a whole community in the controversial establishment of a cheese-factory. With the launching of the great project the life of every inhabitant seems to become activated, if not coarsened. Reason and co-operation will, of course, in the end prevail, and so Gotthelf can freely indulge his narrative imagination and unleash the worst as well as the best proclivities of man. Gotthelf's immense knowledge of human nature—Shakespeare in the garb of a village priest, one of the earliest critics called him— shows here to best advantage; the village expands into a miniature state which mirrors many of the difficulties and triumphs we associate with larger social and political activities. In our context of a peasant literature projecting its own mythology into the nineteenth century *Die Käserei* stands out as a positive contribution to social vision, free from the tendency—to which Gotthelf later succumbs— to keep socialism at bay and lean heavily on conservative forces. It was this undercurrent of hostility to liberal and egalitarian ideas which so often tainted peasant literature with an increasingly reactionary disrepute and turned its mythology into an outdated or at any rate into a marginal phenomenon in German civilization.

At the height of his creative powers Gotthelf emerges as a representative figure, speaking for a world in which the varnish of much that we call culture is of little significance when seen against the basic requirements of human existence: a sensible accounting for the gifts entrusted to us by God, the wonder of being alive, and a conscience that can feel at ease in the knowledge that we have done everything possible to help others in their striving towards human dignity. Concurrently his artistic performance was, in his best years, of the highest order and of a kind that fascinates even where we cannot accept his message as more than a primeval eruption of a passionate concern for mankind.

In addition to the novels we have mentioned there are others which have given new meaning to the term 'Volksliteratur'. The qualification does not pertain to relaxed artistic standards, but to the realistic scene, to problems that are commonly understood and to a spiritual mentorship which we respect for its honesty and simplicity. *Anne Bäbi Jowäger* (1843-44) was begun with the intention of lashing the medical quacks and their stupid victims, but the novel penetrates to deeper levels of human motivation, where superstition borders on relics of old beliefs. It tries to spread enlightenment where obscurantism and the tyranny of unbending characters reign. Needless to say, the events created and described take us through many layers of everyday experience and once more evoke a variety of moods, from unmitigated tragedy to liberating humour. The same applies to *Der Geldstag* (1845), an early experiment in analytic narration, using a bankruptcy sale as the means for illustrating the causes leading to the final dissolution of a once prosperous household. While we accept in this case the moral lesson, we are less willing to attribute much blame for the deplorable state of affairs to the eclipse of conservative principles, as Gotthelf does in *Zeitgeist und Bernergeist* (1852), or to contamination with socialistic ideas as in *Jakobs Wanderungen* (1846-47).

For some readers Gotthelf's novellas and tales are his supreme achievement. There is no loss of significant meaning in them, and often a surprising gain in formal distinction. *Die schwarze Spinne* (1842) has in recent years found such wide acclaim that by a perversion inherent in the *métier* some critics began extolling *Das Erdbeeri Mareili* (1851), *Elsi, die seltsame Magd* (1843), and *Käthi die Grossmutter* (1847), even more enthusiastically. The game can be continued, for there are other gems to choose from, and *Hansjoggeli der Erbvetter* (1848) should by no means be excluded, that delightful tale of an old village philosopher and kind-hearted bachelor who with firmness and humour wards off a number of greedy would-be heirs to his fortune and sees to it that his trusted maidservant is the recipient. Competition and comparison with it will only enhance the beauty of the *Schwarze Spinne*. Set in a contemporary framework, the baptism of a child, an old legend is told that contrasts strongly with the present situation of happiness and peace of mind. The legend takes us back to the days of corruption and temptation by the Devil. The farmers, whom he has helped, try to cheat him out of the promised reward, an unbaptized child, bringing untold misery on the country in the form of a plague of spiders, whose contact first with animals and later with human beings proves deadly. It is assumed that memories of medieval plagues congealed into these terrifying images of death-bringing creatures. To underline the lesson all the more, we hear of a second coming of this plague, when wantonness and lack of obedience to God became rampant again, and, to be sure, in the very house where narrator and listeners are now being entertained. When the guests leave for home they all feel confirmed in their belief that humility, kindness and similar virtues are not hollow words but the very forces which will make or destroy communal life. The interrelation between the events contained in the setting and those told by the grandfather-narrator is both close and natural, and spiritual realities are evoked which transcend all boundaries of time.

Gotthelf's elemental powers of narration make him a towering figure in any methodological context. John Ruskin, who wrote the preface to an English translation of *Uli der Knecht*, published in 1888, concurred in the comparison to Shakespeare to which we referred. Professor H. M. Waidson, the author of the first English study of the Swiss novelist, a searching and comprehensive analysis, says of his work that 'it leads both to an association with figures in Swiss or German regional works and with writers of universally acknowledged calibre like Scott, Dickens or Tolstoy.' This evaluation supports our thesis of Gotthelf's entering upon a new kind of fiction and staking, almost single-handed, a claim for a self-sustained world of mythological dimensions. He did this with the skill of an undisputed master and, if we are to accept Walter Muschg's interpretation of Gotthelf, as a medium through which primordial myth predating Christianity experienced its epiphany. It was fortunate that the Gotthelf renaissance of our time, mainly attributable to Muschg and Werner Günther and since continued by Karl Fehr, began a few years, or a few months, before National Socialist critics, for devious and extraneous reasons, made bold to palm off Gotthelf as a greater figure than even Goethe. What at best could have been a juxtaposition was turned into competition. We are grateful enough that Gotthelf expanded the range of literary awareness to regions which Goethe had to leave out of consideration. If we try to associate Gotthelf with the projection of a mythology, a communion of thought and feeling, of shared ethical and metaphysical beliefs, we notice, by contrast, his many limitations—the place of the sciences, so important for Goethe, was never a consideration for Gotthelf, any more than other aspects in Goethe's cultural orbit. This does not relegate Gotthelf to a more primitive level, though perhaps to the role of a more elementary and elemental teacher, of a man for whom first things—our ethical involvements—come first. It is once again a case of Goethe and—this time not Schiller but Gotthelf. The German scene, if it was to receive adequate literary coverage, needed both, as it needed successors to both, for while Gotthelf's peasant literature was not to achieve a controlling influence over German life, a combination of the two, Goethe's cultural humanism and Gotthelf's practical humanism, might well have become—and in the hopes of some still will become—such a dominant power. The hope is all the more legitimate, because Austrian literature and bourgeois literature appear to be natural allies, just as Marxist mythology, to the extent that it promulgates hopes of a millennium, shows many points of contacts with all of the groups mentioned.

Independently of the Swiss novelist a series of German writers focused their attention on the rural scene. The Black Forest was the background for Berthold Auerbach's (1812–82) *Schwarzwälder Dorfgeschichten* (1843–54), with its peasant life providing an object lesson for a healthy physical and moral life. The paradigmatic case, then and now, is that of a city dweller, preferably an anaemic intellectual, who first considers the village an unbearable exile, only to come more and more under the spell of its regenerative powers. In *Die Frau Professorin* (1846), a novel that engendered a series of literary discussions concerning the advisability of marriage between people of different social classes, Auerbach set out to conquer, through an unspoiled child of nature, the degenerate life of the court. He returned, with *Die Geschichte des Diethelm von Buchenberg* (1853), to the peasant novel in the more restricted sense. Comparison with Gotthelf has unjustly cast on Auerbach the aspersion that he is exploiting a fashion and sugar-coating the realities of peasant life—having no earthy contacts with it as did the pastor of Lützelflüh. But as the son of a Württemberg village pedlar he had had ample opportunity to gain experience of the milieu, and we can just as well argue that he is merely different from and in some respects superior to Gotthelf. For his interests went beyond the horizon of the country-side, and as a socially and politically wide-awake liberal he ventured to survey society as a whole and even to involve his characters in international affairs—the liberation of the North American slaves—in his novel *Das Landhaus am Rhein* (1869). To all his problems he applied the sound judgement of a man brought up in the ethical code of simple country probity. This, and his activities as editor of the *Deutsche Volkskalender*, made him an influential promoter of popular literature. If he was inclined to see in his peasants the heirs of Rousseau and to plead for a new back-to-nature movement, he could also bring his clear and generous thinking to bear on modern social problems; in the pamphlet *Das Judentum und die neueste Literatur* (1836) he put in a strong word for tolerance and equality and deplored petty bourgeois mentality. With Auerbach peasant literature made its boldest forays into adjacent areas of culture and its most energetic bid for the permeation of German life with what many believed to be the rejuvenating naturalness of the rural mind.

Further to the south, straddling Württemberg and Bavarian territory, a district called Ries had in Melchior Meyr (1810–71) a narrator who mirrors in gentle hues the loveliness of this rolling country, bordered by wooded hills, and introduces us to the farmers working and enjoying it. *Erzählungen aus dem Ries* (1856–59) and the hexameters of his verse epic *Wilhelm und Rosina* (1835) are by any standards first-rate literature, but like so many regional works also an invitation to the reader to enter their home ground as if it were a sort of literary tourist resort which we leave exhilarated, but not changed in any specific way. At best, such works have helped other writers who are not of the peasant observance to gain real insight into country life and use their knowledge. The infiltration of peasant literature into the bourgeois sphere can, of course, be observed at many points.

The peasant scene is, for obvious reasons, an integral part of the Austrian literary tradition. It may well be that the wider context in which peasant literature is written in Austria, the problems treated by it, and the social strata involved account for its more national, or better, universal character. Peter Rosegger (1843–1918) serves to illustrate the case. Such earlier works as *Die Schriften des Waldschulmeisters* (1875) and *Waldheimat* (1877) are charming fictional autobiographies of a poor country lad who by dint of hard work and innate talent became a widely read novelist. His education—largely self-provided—and broad interests enabled him to go far beyond narrowly rural concerns and to comment on problems of religion and education, on social and political questions, projecting a co-operation of all classes in the spirit of an earthbound and at the same time joyfully optimistic humanism. However, he misses hardly an opportunity to sing the praises of simple country life and recommend a return to its serene and neighbourly spirit. His ambitious philosophical novels *Der Gottsucher* (1883) and *Welt-gift* (1903) affect a prophetic and hieratic style which suggests that peasant literature is now ready to aspire to an all-embracing myth-ology with an extensive thought-structure. Rosegger came honestly by such a grand vision of a culture arising from rural foundation, but the time was fast approaching when the artificially mythologized peasant world of his countryman Karl Heinrich Waggerl, and of the Germans Friedrich Griese and Hans Friedrich Blunck, made all such simplifications look unreal and sentimental.

In North Germany peasant literature was to assume a very specific character. Its motifs were drawn from a great range of society, and included the inhabitants of the small towns as well. It may have been this more extensive coverage of people and districts which prompted some North German writers to use dialect. There is here none of the indecision of Gotthelf and his mixing of High German with Bernese Alemannic. The language restriction, to which Fritz Reuter (1810–74), John Brinckman (1814–70), and Klaus Groth (1819–99) submitted, discouraged readers who did not speak Low German, but attracted all classes of people within the Low German sphere, simple as well as sophisticated. This literature was not, as we have said, influential enough to lead to the use of the dialect in schools, courts, and churches, and so the readers formed a truly unique literary community, brought together principally by their admiration for Fritz Reuter. 'Few writers,' Gustav Freytag said of him, 'are granted such an effective immortality as his was.' Not surprisingly Low Germans regard the devotion they feel for him and the attraction he exercises on them as something reminis-cent of an ancient society gathered around the poet and drawing sustenance from his words, something akin to the state of affairs in

Homeric times. Reuter's life gave him the advantage of varied interests and experiences, with the central theme of a democratic vision. As a student he was arrested by the authorities who suspected him of liberal activities; a death sentence was commuted into life-long detention, of which he served seven years in various places. Unable to resume his studies after his release, he turned to farming and later to teaching.

He produced with a verse narrative, *Kein Hüsung* (1858), a first work of great beauty and lasting appeal; peasant literature here resumed the role of social accusation that had distinguished a number of Gotthelf's works, and the tragic overtones in it disproved once and for all the contention that dialect writing will invariably veer towards the comical. A rich landowner forbids his servant-girl to marry one of his farm-hands, as he has his own improper designs on her. Exploited to the point of physical exhaustion the lad, in his anger, kills his tormentor and flees to the United States. The girl stays behind with her child, to die in a demented and desperate condition. Years later the father returns to take his boy with him to the free world of America which here, as so often in nineteenth-century literature, beckons as a symbol of a liberty that is actually attainable.

His protest hurled at a greedy and brutal overlord, Reuter settled down to three autobiographical narratives and established his reputation as a great novelist with a wide-awake interest in the realities of life and its social short-comings, though at the same time eager to balance the ills of existence with its no less real joys and satisfactions. *Ut de Franzosentid* (1859) depicts conditions during the French occupation; *Ut mine Festungstid* (1862) recapitulates, with a fairness that is often forgiveness, the now harrowing now comforting days of his incarceration: and *Ut mine Stromtid* (1862–64) collects in a novelistic composition Reuter's experiences as a farmer. The three books have earned him the title of a German Dickens; the last-named work, with its unforgettable Onkel Bräsig, an itinerant inspector and pearl of a man, justifies such a title.

Reuter's most notable gift is the ability to create characters. Some he took from the shelves of literature, and revived them to a new existence, others he found in the towns and villages he stayed in; they acquire, under his sympathetic treatment, a strong enough profile to populate the memories of generations. For plot he did not have to strain his imagination either. Life as he had come to know it supplied him abundantly; moreover, his deft realism could discern in the daily chores of farm life a wealth of captivating details, animated conversations and a series of the most diversified moods. Yet the lasting impression is that of a world at ease, attuned to nature and a home for all those who are willing to exert themselves and practise the tenets of sincere humaneness. Inevitable flaws and mishaps can be absorbed by a tranquil and serene disposition, while unavoidable tragedies must be regarded as inherent in existence and borne with fortitude. Christian love will, however, do most to make life bearable. Reuter is on occasion almost too prone to idealize and to assume the emergence of a social structure in which class differences cease to play a major role and brotherly love regulates the course of human affairs.

He wrote the Low German he had learned in childhood, with some slight concessions to High German. For these he was taken to task by Klaus Groth, no mean lyrical poet, whose *Quickborn* (1852) owes much to Johann Peter Hebel and Robert Burns. Groth was ambitious enough to think of Low German as being in every respect equal, if not superior, to High German as a literary medium. But while his lyrical collection did enchant all Low German regions, from Holland to the Baltic East, he found no followers for his purist views, and no one else has since tried to make the use of dialect so general and exclusive as virtually to segregate the literary culture of North Germany from that of the other parts of the country.

The subject of peasant life is as inexhaustible as that of any other large and compact group, and with the impetus given by Gotthelf and Auerbach regional writing began to spread over the whole of Germany, Austria and Switzerland. Writers of less talent—or of none at all—kept available a steady supply of 'Bauernerzählungen'. Austria made a particularly valuable contribution through Ludwig Anzengruber (1839–89). A second flowering of the genre came towards the end of the century. The threat of economic doom for farmers drove Wilhelm von Polenz (1861–1903) to present in *Der Büttnerbauer* (1895) a dramatic picture of the struggle between a once prosperous farmer and the ruthless speculators exploiting his shortage of cash, first by lending money on horrendous terms and then by taking possession of the mortgaged land. Tolstoy and Zola inspired von Polenz to give his rural *J'accuse* a powerful moral thrust and gripping detail. Lenin is said to have read the novel with great interest, taking it as exposing capitalism at its worst and teaching the irrefutable lesson that the counter-measures of such good-natured but conservative farmers are wholly inadequate and cry for radical political reforms. In Switzerland the oppostion was not so much between an agrarian economy and capitalism as between a tourist industry and a farming community which wished to be left alone, undisturbed by noisy hotels and smoking locomotives. Still, there was enough land left to run the plough through, and peasant literature reverted once more to its time-honoured plots and motifs. Timm Kröger (1844–1918) and Gustav Frenssen (1863–1945) in the North, Jakob Christoph Heer (1859–1925), Ernst Zahn (1867–1952), Alfred Huggenberger (1867–1960), and Hermann Burte (1879–1960) in the Alemannic South and the already mentioned Ludwig Thoma in Bavaria continued to live and work in this rural environment which by now could no longer sustain, as a form of life and a set of common cultural interests, the semblance of a mythology strong enough to leave its imprint on the course of civilization. But with the coming of National Socialism all this was to be changed. 'Blood-and-soil literature', the barbarous term applied to 'Bauerndichtung', was inflated into a mystic concord of absolute values and exemplary forms of life. The very insistence with which the word mythology was applied to peasant life drained the term of all honest significance. For the best qualities of a farmer's existence, such as individuality and independence, and reverence for nature and God, were the last ones which the Germans could aspire to under a cynically authoritarian regime. Typically enough, blood-and-soil language, imagery, and literature soon were compounded with military speech, thus revealing the sham values which the blood-and-soil writers were sometimes naïvely and more often submissively supporting.

7   *The Austrian Tradition*

In 1806 Napoleon by a stroke of his pen put an end to the Holy
Roman Empire; Austria, with other nations, had to find its own
national identity. A number of institutions were bound to assume
a more distinctly Austrian flavour. The nation had long had its
share of writers, but it was only now that they became conscious of
a native tradition and began to emphasize its specific components.
They did not at this early stage indulge in a freer use of their Austro-
Bavarian dialect, but a growing preference for subjects from Austrian life and history is noticeable. This does not in itself make for a
significant and truly representative national literature, much as it
helps in bringing national aspects into higher relief. It has become a
commonplace to relate the salient characteristics of Austrian culture
to the baroque period and to see them shaped by a variety of joyfully pursued human interests and by a tendency to comprehend all
mundane matters *sub specie aeternitatis*. It will be remembered that
Austria under Joseph II (1741–90) enjoyed the most enlightened rule
in all Europe. The spirit of Enlightenment is in many ways complementary to that of baroque, filling as it does the spacious visions of
the latter with a missionary sense of tolerance, peace, mutual understanding. These aims were set high enough to impregnate centuries
of civilization with a belief in a meaningful life. Succeeding generations could subscribe to them and thus gave Austria its well-known
continuity of form and content.

Herbert Eisenreich recently ventured a more detailed characterization of his countrymen, and most of what he says agrees with the
critical consensus. Austrian writers, he tells us, show an obvious
lack of ambition, as far as a direct influence on their readers is concerned; they are as much concerned with political problems as any—
such an interest was a prerequisite of the old Austrian Empire—but
they do not, as the Young Germans did, clamour for action. Connected with this reticence is a marked distrust of grandiloquent
effects; theirs is the belief in Stifter's gentle law, which by the logic
of intelligence and kindness will transform the world. Also, there is a

noticeable bias for concreteness and a concomitant contempt for mere speculation and abstruseness. It is no contradiction of the baroque zest for life when Eisenreich discovers an underlying feeling of sombreness that cautions us not to take the glittering surface too much for granted, but to be prepared for insecurity, sorrow, and death. However, this will not cause Austrian writers to dwell on paralysing anguish—they will merely advise against over-estimating our powers to effect signal progress. We are inclined to put greater emphasis than Eisenreich does on a strong and continuous confession of faith in humanism, Christian or secular, in Austrian literature, a belief that in accordance with the 'gentle law' reality or at any rate society is amenable to a degree of refinement that will warrant our hopes for a life of reason, kindness, and peace.

The wide diffusion of these values in Austrian literature is a striking phenomenon, making for the most readily perceptible and concrete of the four mythologies we have mentioned. In it there are, to be sure, large veins which we have also encountered in peasant and socialist literature and which we shall see again in bourgeois mythology. The wonder of it is that the Austrians were able to impregnate the elements of the other mythologies with their own spirit, or to appropriate them and set them like spokes into the hub of their native culture. This is true of thought as well as of form. Both Austrian socialism and the Austrian peasantry, for instance, were strongly allied with the Christian grounding of their native civilization; and both of them, and the bourgeoisie to an even larger degree, share with the upper classes a great pride and interest in the cultural life of the nation. The style of poetic realism—largely a product of Austrian literature—was the natural form of artistic communication; it survived longer in Austria than anywhere else and subdued, to some extent, the more intransigent features of naturalism and expressionism. Literary historians speak of the Austrian half-expressionists; they might similarly refer to Austrian half-naturalists.

But strong as the assimilative power of the Austrian tradition was, it lacked, as one would expect, the aggressive drive to conquer other German-speaking territories, propitious as the situation for such expansion appeared between 1815 and 1848, during the restoration which was, after all, controlled by Metternich. But then, as Eisenreich points out, Austrians lack aggressiveness; moreover, some of the most typical works of Austrian humanism appeared after the middle of the century, too late to enter Germany in the baggage of Metternich's couriers.

Perhaps the most endogenous strand in the Austrian tradition is the Viennese popular theatre, the 'Vorstadtbühnen' that catered for a middle- and lower-class clientele, providing good entertainment sprinkled with moral precepts. These popular plays combined two traditions: the Jesuit drama of the baroque period with its endeavour to render religious instruction more palatable by serving it in dramatic form, and the *commedia dell' arte*, with its set of easily identifiable types that can be conveniently adjusted to local conditions. Farce, fairy tale, and the harlequin, all banished from the German stage by the purist Gottsched and his successors, re-entered the stage in Germany through the backdoor of the Viennese 'Volkstheater'. But this was not to take place until late in the nineteenth century, and meanwhile anyone craving for spectacular drama, hilariously funny or mysteriously imaginative plays had to travel to Vienna. He need not worry about variety and would have his choice from three types of drama, fairy-tale pieces, slapstick comedy and parody. What turned a local product originating in the eighteenth century all of a sudden into great literature was the accident of two men of genius appearing on the scene as actors, directors, and playwrights. Ferdinand Raimund (1790–1836) and Johann Nepomuk Nestroy (1801–62) have left a repertoire that is as alive today as it was in their own times. The Horatian *aut docere aut delectare* is here followed to perfection. Neither of the two was simply a funny man—pushing action and conversation from one joke to another—German literature does not know this type of writer. Their seriousness was relished as much as their humour.

Raimund strikes one as more refined than Nestroy—but this is a judgement of style and imagination, not of intrinsic value. He hews closer to an idealistic tradition fond of conjuring up all sorts of spirits who would, like the gods of Homer, interest themselves in some mortal man and support his works, good and evil. The end of the struggle is hardly ever in doubt, nor is it decided by a *deus ex machina*. The protégé has to give proof of his moral superiority. Nestroy was more of a realist and soon discarded the aid and interference of fancifully conceived spirits; instead, he makes the constitution of man the sole source of his deeds and fate. There are no more eerie spirits to speak in lofty words. Raimund commanded a language that was lyrical and musical enough to make simple truth sound fresh and convincing, and though a keen observer of human behaviour and superbly gifted in making set characters look like native originals, his preference is for plots and temperaments which can be ennobled and idealized.

The conflicts are nevertheless earthy and traditional; time makes no difference, human beings will for ever exhibit the same foibles and virtues, nor does our moral evaluation of them change. Neither Hegel's philosophy of history nor Schopenhauer's metaphysics seem to have dented the Austrian structure of thought; if there is progress it will always be determined and measured by the quality of human thought and action. No plea to take refuge from the world in a state of non-being can prevent normal people from enjoying life and trying to make the best of it. Finally, there is a general consensus about the scale of lasting values, with serenity, love, tolerance heading the list. In a broad sense it is the ethics of Christian humanism which keep society in peace and harmony. To act as guardians of these values Raimund invents his own mythological figures, kind spirits drawn from the Indian, Austrian or any other sky. By and large, Raimund's world is *naturaliter humana*, and if the plays written for the Viennese popular playhouses addressed themselves to a restricted audience, linguistically speaking, this audience was given to understand that the basic issues and problems of existence are the same everywhere, leading to virtually identical conflicts and responding to the same solutions. Raimund's characters may be archetypes in the final analysis, but not until they have done some undressing: dirndl costumes, knee-breeches, and Tyrolese hats give them a strongly regional flavour.

Raimund wrote his first play for his own 'Benefizabend' as an actor at the 'Leopoldstädter Theater'. The comedian turned playwright caused no mean sensation, success surpassed all expectations, and *Der Barometermacher auf der Zauberinsel* (1823) was to hold its place among the four or five masterpieces Raimund has left. The work is based on a fairy-tale written by a German serving at the court of Weimar; Raimund, like Nestroy and other purveyors of dramatic fare, felt no pangs of conscience when filching his plots wherever he spotted them, knowing that such pilfering would barely be noticeable in the final product. The story that he used treats of a Prince Tutu. Among the things left to him by his father there is an ebony chest containing an empty purse that will fulfil any wish, a small horn which can conjure up whole armies, and a belt that provides rapid transportation. The prince is now hopeful that he can win the heart of Princess Zenomide, the glamorous but cruel daughter of Shah Abukaf. Zenomide covets the purse more than the heart of its owner, and manages to steal it. To recover it Tutu places himself at the head of an army. Zenomide feigns regret for the theft and succeeds in stealing the magic horn as well. With the belt that makes one invisible Tutu enters Zenomide's bedroom, to force the surrender of the other two objects. Needless to say, he leaves minus his belt. Attempting suicide, dangling from a fig tree and eating its fruit he notices that with each fig his nose grows by an inch, as a punishment, he thinks for his gullibility. When he drinks from a nearby well the nose shrinks to normal size. Tutu, putting two and two together, can now arrange for his revenge. Dressed as a pedlar he comes to court and sells his figs to the princess who, exasperated by her growing nose, offers to hand back the stolen goods to anyone who can cure her—time for Tutu to step forward, in the garb of a physician, and regain his magic objects.

Raimund both parodies the legend and turns the parody into a self-sufficient comedy. Colourless Tutu is transformed into a type of universal occurrence—though the Viennese are convinced that he is a distinctly local character—into the happy-go-lucky fellow, resourceful and good-humoured, who starts as the underdog and moves to great affluence, without hurting anybody except those who hurt him. To toss a shipwrecked Viennese barometer-maker into such an exotic and magic-ridden island is the initial spark that starts a wildfire of both precarious and humorous situations, lively conversations and quick-witted repartee. Since tradition required that Fortunatus must return not only a wealthy man, but also as a happy lover or husband, Raimund has a second set of events going, with his hero's slow realization that Linda and not the princess is the girl of his destiny—Linda as the chamber-maid of the evil woman helps her countryman in his plight and returns with him as his sweetheart Linderl.

The didactic ingredients of the original tale are not discarded but refined, becoming an unobtrusive demonstration of God helping those who help themselves. A brief opening scene assists the audience in grasping the deeper meaning of the play, and we notice this ethical thread even when we are moved to tears of laughter by the brisk march of events or the clash between Viennese dialect and the courtly stiffness of High German. When the curtain rises, we see an assembly of nymphs and a fairy called Rosalinde. She is the keeper of the three magic objects and commissioned to place them every hundred years in the hands of a worthy person. But who nowadays deserves to be happy? Serious claimants are few and far between, and more often than not they disappoint the board of judges with their coarse materialism. Nor are the latter certain that a barometer-maker— his name is Quecksilber—whom they choose more by accident than by conviction, will give a good account of himself. Only time can tell, and so the examination starts, with the audience watching in deep suspense. That the examinee will pass is not a foregone conclusion, as in Goethe's *Faust*, for an ordinary man like Quecksilber, now in possession of the means to grant himself every wish, might easily go to seed. It is only when Linda enters his life that we feel reassured—he is basically too decent a person to disappoint such an honest child of nature.

Das Mädchen aus der Feenwelt oder Der Bauer als Millionär (1826), *Der Alpenkönig und der Menschenfeind* (1828) and *Der Verschwender* (1834) vie with *Der Barometermacher* in popularity. The blending of the comical with the tragic, of everyday reality with the mysterious powers behind it, appears in each of these plays in a new constellation, to deal with different yet invariably vital problems, intelligible to everybody and vividly personified by flesh and blood characters. The farmer turned millionaire, who all but fails the test to which he is subjected—to remain or to become again a decent human being; the misanthrope who mends his ways after a cleverly staged and psychologically most expert confrontation with his own unbearable character, impersonated by a sly and well-meaning servant; the spendthrift, light-hearted and generous, but in Raimund's eyes nevertheless guilty of not using his gifts intelligently for the well-being of his fellow-men, but who in the end will be saved from ruin because of one act of true kindness that has accumulated enough interest, in moral and financial coin, to make restitution for his guilt and replace his monetary losses—these are the plots and characters with which Raimund regales us delightfully and instructs us. In the final analysis the struggle is between timeless values and a 'Zeitgeist' that tempts us to pooh-pooh the warnings of our conscience. Yet Raimund—and the same is true of Nestroy—confesses to a belief in the continuous reappearance of reasonable and warm-hearted men and women, presenting as he does in every play some shining and at the same time realistically drawn instance of human valour, most frequently found among simple farmers and trades-people.

Being so close to Platonism, to a vision of immutable values which demand embodiment in reality and mobilization against the base instincts in human nature, Raimund must have felt tempted to give some monumental expression to the battle between good and evil. *Moisasurs Zauberfluch* (1827) has been called the Austrian *Faust*, and as long as the emphasis is left on the Austrian half of the term the allusion to Goethe is permissible. One of Raimund's contemporaries expressed the fear that the involvement of a vast array of extramundane powers representing a range of absolute values with 'the forms and manifestations of the ordinary hustle and bustle of bourgeois life' was too great a risk. But the risk paid, and the audience was willing to explore with Raimund the fount and origin of the ideas that govern all human activities, and those of the carefree Viennese as well. Like his predecessors, Karl Meisl (1775–1853), Adolf Bäuerle (1786–1859) and others, Raimund invented his own mythology to illustrate his philosophy. The Indian Queen Alzinde makes an unequivocal declaration for Virtue and against the messenger of evil, Moisasur. The latter orders the temple of Alzinde to be razed, to show the world how powerless religion and ethics have become. The design fails, Virtue emerges triumphant. Moisasur now turns everything in the land into stone, and Alzinde into an ugly beggar-woman. There is however a limit to Moisasur's influence—it will cease on the day that Alzinde is found in the arms of death, weeping tears of joy. The meaning of this condition is plain—he who can face death serenely must have lived a good life and be-

D

lieved in a benign deity. Alzinde's trial begins by her being whisked away into a region familiar to the Viennese audiences, the Austrian country-side. The farmer Gluthahn, whom she, young and hopeful in spirit but ugly in body, begs for help, turns her cruelly away, and with such and similar encounters it is small wonder that despair takes hold of her. What saves her from self-destruction is the knowledge of and faith in her own spirit, a clear refutation of man's inhumanity. Also, there is the imperishable splendour of nature to bolster her courage. The reward comes when Hans and Mirzel appear on the scene, two simple, contented souls, who take pity on the destitute woman. Moved by such charity, Alzinde weeps tears that turn into diamonds. Gluthahn on hearing about it lures her away, to sell the producer of such treasures to a jeweller in the city.

At the opening of the second act we find the jeweller Rossi nursing some doubts as to the propriety of the deal suggested by Gluthahn. The case is taken to court, and while the witnesses are being interrogated Raimund provides for the needed comic relief. The judge is an honest man doing his best to unmask Gluthahn, but he is also a pedant and rationalist; he suspects Alzinde of witchcraft and wants to punish her for it. The poor woman is thrown into gaol, but remains unbroken in spirit, fortified by a clear conscience. Death comes to tempt her with the promise of peace, but in the nick of time her husband King Hoanghu appears to barter with Death and offer half of his life span for hers. Overwhelmed by such love, Alzinde weeps in the embrace of Death and creates the situation that is to terminate Moisasur's evil reign.

The play has been properly interpreted as Raimund's almost frantic attempt to warn a world enslaved by materialism that it must heed some fundamental verities. He does this with all the spiritual resources of the baroque tradition. The same reminder was to be given again by Hofmannsthal, notably in the last version of *Der Turm* (1927). Meanwhile the secularization which Raimund dreaded continued, and it fell to Nestroy to cope with this development and to do what he could to keep it controlled within the Austrian tradition. For this he enlisted the powers of irony and sarcasm. His contemporaries could not fail to notice the change and to sense a chill sent down their spines by Nestroy. Critics called him the Mephistopheles of the 'Volksstück', the dramatist who sounded its death-knell. Gone were the days and plays of supernatural beings playing guardian angel for their mortal friends. Virtue, Hope, and Vice no longer appeared in person, their qualities now resided in the characters of men, and these had to work out their own salvation. As Friedrich Schlögel in his reminiscences *Vom Wiener Volkstheater* (1883) says, 'all of a sudden the city of carefree life was showered with a rain of infernal sulphurous wit, flooded with a corroding acid and a hurricane of dialectical verbiage, a lava-stream of merciless controversies broke into the flower garden of intimate feelings and romantic dreams.' But if Nestroy did all this, he did it as one who always knew where to discover 'the electric spot from which, if properly rubbed, the sparks of hilarity will jump off'.

The difference between Raimund and Nestroy shows in the very medium they were working in. For Raimund language is a mysteriously and adequately pliable means to express thoughts and feelings; he can make it serve a comical situation, or a loftily lyrical one, while the pun on words, or words allowed to play with words, occur rarely. Nestroy on the other hand goes out of his way to make the word work as much as it can; association proliferates words, forcing the speaker to run after them to regain control; a slight twist to an expression and it reveals unexpected vistas of reality; a slip of the tongue, and the result seems to corroborate Freud long before he appeared on the scene. Nestroy's language is active to the point of being unpredictably explosive, allowed either to short-circuit or to run along a quick-match. It is for good reasons that studies of his word-artistry are numerous and in agreement on his kinship with Morgenstern and Ringelnatz, as well as with modern attempts to liberate the word from its traditional task of being rationally meaningful. Yet with all his dash in stirring the word to independent action Nestroy remains in control of plot and meaning, and dissolution into a fragmentary reality is prevented by the endeavour to interpret life and impose normative thoughts, feelings, and forms of behaviour. If the words play cat and mouse with each other and the boundaries between sense and nonsense become blurred, this is all done in a still playful mood which fits well into the baroque tradition.

His first signal success, after a number of minor works, *Der böse Geist Lumpazivagabundus oder Das liederliche Kleeblatt* (1833) indicated the specifications of his gifts—they took him away from the 'Märchen- und Zauberspiel' and in the direction of the 'realistische Besserungsstück', of 'Charaktergemälde und Sittenstück', as the local terminology has it. Needless to say, literary parody was a sideline in which he was destined to shine—his *Judith und Holofernes* (1849), parodying Hebbel's *Judith*, *Tannhäuser* (1857) and *Lohengrin* (1859) are model specimens of this genre.

If, according to Eisenreich, in Nestroy's world 'God no longer acts upon an existence that has become wholly self-dependent, with depravity set free', there was still the author to make his ideas and wishes felt, and Nestroy did so as a man of liberal thought and sympathy with the downtrodden. While many of his more than eighty plays had to supply a fast-changing repertoire he managed to speak his own mind in a number of them—they have survived for this reason and fortunately also for their formal distinction.

Zu ebener Erde und erster Stock oder Die Launen des Glücks (1835) takes in plot and technical execution a step towards social drama. A rich family occupying an upper apartment and a poor one living downstairs keep two sets of action going simultaneously. A sudden change, unexpected riches entering below and fortune leaving above with the tenants moving accordingly—such a picture would speak for itself even if the two milieus were not connected by many threads. What we still miss is an explicit reference to the origin of poverty in a system that allows and promotes inequality. Came 1848, and Nestroy, in *Freiheit in Krähwinkel*, went where his stabs at a degenerate nobility and a ruthless set of *nouveaux riches* had long shown him to belong. Ever since Kotzebue's *Die deutschen Kleinstädter* (1803) small-town life had been the butt of political satire, with a devout, spineless bourgeoisie kotowing to genuine or pretended nobility. Daring the ubiquitous threat of Austrian censorship Nestroy restaged the revolution, covering the reactionaries with ignominy and equipping the revolutionaries with the deadly weapon of satire and the irresistible force of a righteous cause. But, great artist that he was, in justice to truth he did not spare his rebellious characters from ridicule for their lack of reason and vision. Simple souls wondered which side he was on, after all, and intelligent men among his critics accused him of having engaged in persiflage against the efforts of gallant fighters for freedom. Yet all he wanted to emphasize was that a passionate heart had to be paired with a cool mind, if reforms were to be enacted instead of just loudly proclaimed, that fervent idealism must be tempered with thoughtful realism. About his involvement in the cause of liberalism there can be no doubt. *Der alte Mann mit der jungen Frau* (1849) ridiculed the persecution of beaten and scattered revolutionaries; one of them wins the sympathy of an aristocrat, who helps him to escape to Australia, and thus to save his energies for the next round in the social struggle.

This clear decision in favour of social change brought the wrath of the censors down on the playwright. He could no longer send his men into battle or make others applaud them on their way. Instead, he created a number of characters, men and women, who practise a rare kindness and humility, though with the occasional vitriolic comment on the established social order. In *Kampl oder Das Mädchen mit Millionen und die Nähterin* (1852) the suburban medical practitioner Kampl is the personification of both Austrian humanity and humanism, clever and witty, close to the common man and never afraid of criticizing the compact majority, but most of all a man of never-failing kindness, the friend of his usually indigent patients to whom he doesn't send bills himself and whose bills with the pharmacist he pays. With a penetrating eye for hollowness and false pretences Kampl clears the atmosphere wherever he happens to be; what is most remarkable is the fact that he cannot tell a lie nor hide the truth. Yet with all his seemingly naïve outspokenness Nestroy refrained from creating in Kampl merely a means for provoking comical situations out of the clash between social convention and simplicity of mind. No matter how much the author uses Kampl to expose our sham values, he does not abuse him for the sake of cracking jokes. The humorist is held in check by the social thinker.

For similar plays in which Nestroy invents a plot or reshapes a borrowed one, to produce either hilarious fireworks, or bitter comments on the human predicament—quite often the two go hand in hand—we can turn to *Das Mädl aus der Vorstadt oder Ehrlich währt am längsten* (1841), *Einen Jux will er sich machen* (1842), *Liebesgeschichten und Heiratssachen* (1843), and *Der Zerrissene* (1844). The last is, of course, a parody on the psychological malaise discovered by Young Germany, the blasé attitude of a mind that feels torn by conflicting interests and excused for its inactivity. The patient in

Nestroy's case is a man of means, but without energy. We can foresee that he will be contrasted with simple working people, who have no time for and no understanding of such ailments. This kind of unhappy disposition is hard to comprehend in a man who drinks so much wine, one of the servants remarks, whereupon another answers: 'This you don't understand; he has a torn soul, the wine runs through it but cannot get to his head.' And now it is the turn of the first one to exclaim: 'A torn soul with all that money!'

The Viennese popular stage of Raimund and Nestroy and their predecessors is not a miniature of the Austrian tradition, rather its metropolitan expression, nourished by the life of Vienna and its people, who are intelligent and unsentimental and who yet possess a great capacity to experience emotions, whether servant or master, coachman or nobleman. The popular plays that were written for them, and written with their assistance, with the characters they offered for portrayal, have resulted in a unique cultural phenomenon. They have hardly ever been given due consideration in histories of literature that set their course by Goethe and Schiller but have usually been relegated to the level of Austrian folk-art. In recent years, when German dramatists have tried to imitate Nestroy's and Raimund's thoughts and tricks—Dürrenmatt called the Viennese popular stage the most attractive phenomenon of the German-speaking theatre—a deeper and more appreciative evaluation is evident and faint attempts in Germany to establish an equally lively and captivating tradition are recorded with satisfaction. There is much to be made up. From Ernst Elias Niebergall's (1815–43) comedy *Des Burschen Heimkehr oder Der tolle Hund* (1837) and his satirical presentation of the petty bourgeois in *Datterich* (1841) to Carl Zuckmayer's *Der fröhliche Weinberg* (1925) German dramatists were in no mood to create and German audiences were not relaxed enough to enjoy characters less strenuous than 'those unbending figures which chill the air of many a play and novel from Hebbel to Hauptmann,' as J. P. Stern puts it. Local dialect drama in Switzerland and elsewhere must be exempted from this verdict, but also from serious literary attention.

Franz Grillparzer (1791–1872) ranks with Hebbel as the outstanding dramatist of the middle of the nineteenth century. Like the latter he came in the wake of German classicism, which he too tried to bend to his own needs. In most other respects Grillparzer and Hebbel were quite different personalities, and though they lived in the same city—Hebbel came to Vienna in 1843, to stay there for the rest of his life—they avoided each other's company and conversation. Grillparzer, for all his contacts with German classicism, was a profound admirer of Raimund. Immersed in the local theatrical conventions, he aspired to a blending of the two traditions, Vienna and Weimar. By comparison Hebbel was an intellectual writer with no patience for the wayward and discursive local drama. If Grillparzer's début with a 'Schicksalstragödie', *Die Ahnfrau* (1817), was an obvious bow in the direction of the hair-raising thriller, his next play, *Sappho* (1818), was hailed by the German guardians of high style as belonging to their sphere. This was the work that made Byron say of Grillparzer: 'a devil of a name, but we shall have to take notice of it.' The play's motif and its philosophical implications place *Sappho* in the lineage of works dealing with the artist in conflict with society, with Goethe's *Tasso* (1789), Thomas Mann's *Tonio Kröger* (1903) and Carl Spitteler's *Imago* (1906). Yet the incisive handling of the problem and the final verdict that great art is incompatible with the enjoyment of ordinary life is embedded in such exciting drama, with daggers drawn and lovers pursued across the Aegean, that the theatre-goer demanding a spectacle rather than a philosophical discussion received his share as well. If anything, Grillparzer had to be on his guard to keep the play level on its tragic keel and to refrain from delivering Sappho to those spectators who hoped to see the aging woman comically treated in her frantic effort to wrest her young lover Phaon from the arms of the more attractive Melitta. His diction elucidates both emotion and reason. The sufferings of Sappho become as real as they are inevitable and involve us in the tragic aspect of the theme without allowing the imagination to distort it into comedy.

Sappho was followed by the trilogy *Das goldene Vlies* (1821), the story of Jason bringing Medea to his native Greece and exposing her to an alien environment in which the two lovers wound each other and become irrevocably estranged. A theme from classical mythology is here developed by a poet who must have witnessed in his own country the risks of transplantation and the clash of an earthbound tradition with a more sophisticated society. With the nineteenth-century Austrian's insight into the mores of other nations, Grillparzer moves freely from *Der Traum ein Leben* (1834), set in a mythical Orient, to the Spain of the Middle Ages in *Die Jüdin von Toledo* (1873) or to Merovingian France in his comedy *Weh' dem, der lügt* (1840). The history of his own people he used to expound themes of great human and political import, nowhere with a greater engagement than in *König Ottokars Glück und Ende* (1825). The play reflects the relief felt after the liberation of Europe from Napoleon, lays bare the immorality of the usurper, and looks hopefully into a peaceful future. Ottokar, the Bohemian king of the thirteenth century who wants to subjugate by war and marriage as many of his neighbours as possible, and finally to reach for the Imperial crown, is enmeshed in his *hubris*, and loses all, including life, in battle against Rudolf von Habsburg. The play ends in tragedy for one who deserved no better. Ottokar by his own admission has ruled badly over his lands—but the final mood and message is one of hopefulness. The path is now cleared for Rudolf to fulfil the dream of Grillparzer's political vision—it is the ideal of all great Austrian writers down to Hofmannsthal and Broch, in harmony with a nation pledged to enlightenment and civilised conduct. There is a ringing proclamation to this effect by Rudolf:

> Die Welt ist da, damit wir alle leben,
> Und gross ist nur der ein' allein'ge Gott!
> Der Jugendtraum der Erde ist geträumt,
> Und mit den Riesen, mit den Drachen ist
> Der Helden, der Gewalt'gen Zeit dahin.
> Nicht Völker stürzen sich wie Berglawinen
> Auf Völker mehr, die Gärung scheidet sich,
> Und nach dem Zeichen sollt' es fast mich dünken,
> Wir stehn am Eingang einer neuen Zeit.

Grillparzer here writes as if the kingdom of God on earth were close at hand, now that the flood of the Napoleonic wars has receded. In Germany Schiller's *Wilhelm Tell*, even before the fall of the tyrant, helps the Swiss peasants back to their simple but free life. Yet *Tell* presents mainly a recovery of rights formerly enjoyed, in the limited sphere of rural society. Austrian writers sketched their projections for peaceful civilization on a much larger scale, taking into consideration a more complex social and national structure. Their own multi-racial homeland left them with no other choice.

Stifter in his introduction to *Bunte Steine* expressed his faith in the same progressive march of historical events: the Golden Age is near; the feeling of solidarity is spreading among all nations; rulers and ruled all benefit equally from the light of reason and the warmth of heart.

Grillparzer's own experience with officials was less satisfactory, and after 1837 he went into self-chosen retreat, shunning all public contacts. But his interest in public affairs did not diminish; in *Ein treuer Diener seines Herrn* (1830), *Libussa* (1872) and *Ein Bruderzwist in Habsburg* (1872) he continued to invoke the forces of reason and compassion against the ever threatening demons of strife and hatred. He did so with grave concern about the possibility of realizing idealistic aims through political devices. What remains unimpaired by the passing of time is his apt use of dramatic effect; the conflicts are embodied in human beings, not in ideological puppets, the sharp political or philosophical issues do not become isolated from throbbing life. He is closer to the drama of presentation, as Otto Ludwig defended it against Hebbel's drama of conflicting ideas, in which the characters are chessmen on the board of a predetermined history of mankind. Ludwig pleaded for the clash of emotions and passions, welling up from deep levels of existence, and Grillparzer keeps repeating in his diaries that the function of art is to provide for a unified emotional experience to which thought and action must be related. He anticipates T. S. Eliot's demand that the poets first of all inform us of the emotional climate of a given period and then try to find normative feelings. Grillparzer records with pride that Austria, in contrast to Germany, is still richly endowed with fresh emotions. The range of his feeling is wide and rich in nuances. Indeed, two of his plays draw their conflicts almost exclusively from elemental passions.

Des Meeres und der Liebe Wellen (1840) shares with Shakespeare's *Romeo and Juliet* the rare quality of being a tragedy of love pure and simple. The more subdued and discreet Grillparzer's love scenes are, the greater the depth of passion. The catastrophe may be not unconnected with adverse circumstances—Leander falls in love with Hero while she is being prepared to take the vows of a priestess—and the final doom may be sealed by an act of inadvertence, as in Hero's falling asleep and failing to keep the lamp burning for her lover, but these acts of an unkind fate leave the poet free to depict a few hours of passion, a paean on youth and love which the sad ending cannot silence. Over Gretchen's love lies the shadow of Mephistopheles from the beginning, and our response to her initial bliss is more that of fear than of happy participation. But the sympathy springing up between Leander and Hero has the innocence of nature, it is whole and wholesome, not endangered by weakness or fickleness; generations of young readers have plunged into this fountain of true love, taking its tragic outcome as accidental rather than inherent. The emotional appeal is strong, an experience which adds to the aesthetic fascination of the play. We feel it in our muscles when Leander swims the straits, and the finest nerves are touched when Hero, before kissing Leander, puts the lamp away.

Der Traum ein Leben (1834) keeps love in the background for the time being, to unleash those other supposedly basic urges of man: ambition, will to power, superiority over other people. Adler's psychology is here foreshadowed and treated as complementary to Freud's. Psycho-analysts have gleefully hailed Grillparzer's play as a corroboration of their theories, and it is indeed as good a cure for ambition run wild as has ever been effected on a couch. Rustan, the country lad of megalomaniac plans, is made to enact in his dreams a ruthless pursuit of power, which pushes him near the brink of crime. On awakening from this vicarious indulgence in power-drunk egotism he can wipe the sweat of the criminal nightmare off his brow and return to the innocent life which in his heart he has always desired, mistakenly thinking that to prove himself worthy of Mirza, his foster-father's daughter, he would have to cover himself with the glory of power. In none of his other plays has Grillparzer borrowed so much from the 'Volkstheater', in the way of exotic scenes, strange apparitions and miraculous *dénouements*— yet with all the pomp and circumstance of theatrical effects he illustrates a conflict of classical significance and simplicity.

A Schillerian way of making antagonists clash head on, a Goethean empathy in penetrating the intimate life of the soul, with such elements Grillparzer brings the development of German classical drama, which started with Lessing and ended with himself and

Hebbel, to another unexpected flowering. Even so, symptoms appear that herald a crisis in dramatic writing which will compel a rest until the naturalists evolve a style more in keeping with modern views and burning social concern. Grillparzer's language, by absorbing larger segments of realism, loses the majestic flow it had had in *Sappho*, as it tends to make metrical forms subservient to a more natural diction, with realistic conversation as its model. Moreover, Grillparzer becomes increasingly aware that the scene on which contemporary conflicts originate is the inner life of an individual rather than the public sphere; ordinary people would seldom have an opportunity or feel the necessity of taking issue with forces outside themselves. Human problems are becoming more private and personal.

For such concerns prose, the prose of fiction and particularly of the novella and short story, forms the adequate literary medium. Grillparzer relished neither prose nor narrative fiction, yet by some stroke of luck gave us *Der arme Spielman* (1848), an undisputed masterpiece in novella-writing. He anticipates some of the questions which were later to be put insistently: what is the narrator's function, what is his place and viewpoint within his tale, and how can he make bold to give shape and meaning to the labyrinthine maze of data which compose a man's life?

Grillparzer, within the compass of sixty pages, manages to say much that he could not reveal within the less subtle structure of drama. It is in this story, as J. P. Stern says, that 'the innermost character of the man, and the true meaning of his experience of life, are disclosed more fully and directly than in any of his dramas.' The story is of a fiddler, told partly by himself and partly by a narrator, a man whose psychological interests make him curious about this street musician who receives only meagre earnings in his hat and leaves when the big crowds arrive, to repair to his garret and to a life of his own, to an inner happiness issuing from a strong and serene heart. His life has been one of constant losses— the care of a well-to-do father, the love of a simple girl, the inheritance that might have made him independent—but as he is reduced to a bare existence he begins to assemble his inner riches.

Music has much to do with this private wealth, not the sordid jumble of grating tunes he treats the passers-by to, but the music he hears, a harmony from above, a divine manifestation of cosmic order and joyfulness. If this is a symptomatic Austrian way of transforming reality, it is also more than the much-vaunted Viennese blend of music and gaiety. For Jacob—this is the fiddler's name—such little skill as he has can serve as the spring-board to an art beyond all human perfection, it is as if the spheres were performing for him, showering him with their harmonies. He experiences what Stifter calls religion in the garb of aesthetic sensation. What the word, not even that of the Bible, cannot do for man is done for him by art, particularly by music. The thought is not strange in a culture like the Austrian baroque which erected in its art a spiritual dome that united and sheltered the most diverse manifestations of creed and race and made them melodies in the chorus of praise for God and his creation.

However, the fiddler's contentment with his lot is more than an aesthetic experience, it issues from a heart that is happy in giving without receiving. By a queer trick of fate the poor man is empowered to give more than the richest people are willing to give, his own life. Not that Grillparzer stages some heroic deed for him, there is rather a touch of irony in the fact that Jacob, on the occasion of a flood, wades into a cellar to save the account-book of a bourgeois acquaintance and thereby catches a fatal illness. This ending accords with the essence of the tale; it is precisely in a humble soul that the cosmic order finds its clearest mirror, and not the greatness of the deed counts, but the spirit from which it emanates.

A quiet individual life and a society made up of such unassuming people, forming themselves in the image of perfect order, this is also the impression created by Stifter's work. Adalbert Stifter (1805–68) reinforces that other component of Austrian culture, the hope for an enlightenment which is complementary to the spacious sphere of baroque acceptance of a pluralistic world. With a modesty and simplicity that contrasts strongly with the complexity of his mind he writes in the prefaces to his two collections of stories, *Studien* (1844) and *Bunte Steine* (1854), that he has no ambition as an artist but would be happy to bring some enjoyment to his reader and to contribute to the strengthening of our moral fibre. We know from his essays how close to his heart this educational purpose was, and that it could be attained only by the moral self-discipline of the artist. His convictions hark back to the Enlightenment as he equates the good an artist can do with the quality of his personal character. Any flaws will show in the works he produces and in turn will adversely affect the reader or spectator. Stifter establishes the most rigorous nexus between artist and art, and between art and its effect. Of all German writers from Gottsched to Thomas Mann who believe in the missionary function of art Stifter has taken the greatest pains to anchor such convictions in the metaphysics of life. God, Providence or whatever it is that watches over the world, needs the artist. We are not coming from but moving into the Golden Age; the time of internecine strife is over and an irresistible urge towards universal solidarity is asserting itself everywhere. Progress depends more on individual than on political action. By the gentle law, 'das sanfte Gesetz', man can conquer his selfish impulses and submit to the requirements of peaceful communal and international existence. The artist, and most of all the writer, is called upon to define the ethos of the community. He will describe test cases in which the gentle law, the application of reason, kindness and patience, succeeds in overcoming mental or emotional inertia. Emotions form the main concern of literature. The poet is in a position to prescribe the feelings that are needed to keep the flow of love, as it emanates from God, moving and diffusing into all of life's channels.

Stifter was not the simple personality such a thought-structure might suggest. We need not refer to his attempted suicide, to confirm the existence of inner turmoil. There are other indications of insecurity and doubt. It was by a resolute fiat of his will that he created his world and decreed it to be the scene on which human beings can confidently work out a meaningful destiny. We must respect this as a deeply ingrained conviction. Its validity is underscored by a number of works in which the hypothesis of the gentle law is shown to work out satisfactorily, in spite of the numerous obstacles that reality throws into the path of moral progress. True, some of his tales leave an unresolved residue: happiness that is not the reward of virtue, and tragedy where there was no lack of regard for the gentle law. And there are vestiges of gloom in many of his works that belie the optimism he proclaimed.

Yet by and large Stifter creates a reality that is susceptible to reason and love. Disorder turned into order, the threat of passion averted by reasonable emotion, these are the fundamental moves on the chess-board of his didactic tales and novels. A measure of wishful thinking and adjusting the hard facts of life to ideal visions may underlie such plots. *Das Heidedorf*, a story from the *Studien*, approaches a mythical dimension, an archetypal dream come true, in which the life of a humble person leads to an exemplary communal order. The son of a heath farmer is subjected in a short space of time to all the impulses necessary for the development of mind and soul, and for the realization of his duty to return home to put his talents at the disposal of his people. Eric Blackall calls the story a miniature 'Entwicklungsroman'; it is also a prefiguration of Stifter's political novel *Witiko*, for the forces that make for a harmonious village are the same that build a peaceful nation.

In the same *Studien* we have *Die Narrenburg* to show us how an enclave of wasteland is conquered and made the centre of thriving social and individual activities. *Hochwald*, on the other hand, waits in vain for a leader to embrace the gentle law; instead, the man we set our hopes on is lost to the passions of war and restless activity, and so the country remains desolate, without a saviour. In *Das alte Siegel* the hero, an officer fighting against Napoleon in the War of Liberation—the last *bellum iustum*, by the way, to which an author of the nineteenth century could send his hero with a good conscience—misses the full realization of his abilities, by applying too rigid a standard of honour to life and love and thereby blinding himself to the true character of the woman he expected to marry. *Der Hagestolz* varies the motif of chaos turning into order in a intriguing way—a bachelor and recluse is prised loose from isolation and misanthropy by the naturalness and amiability of his visiting nephew.

Love and friendship are of course important agents in conditioning man for the task of bringing order into the world. Both, and especially love, may reside in levels so deep that they cannot be reached in a first passionate approach. But with good luck, as in *Brigitta*, grave misunderstandings and even the separation of wife and husband can be bridged—here at the bedside of their son—and a reconciliation be achieved that unites the lovers with greater affection than ever before and, which is just as important, qualifies them for creating order and happiness in a community, small or large.

Husband and wife, even during their separation, never quite lost their respect for each other; and a sense of values untapped at first remains—reason enough to make their paths converge in happiness.

It is less obvious why Abdias, in the story named after him, meets with final unhappiness. His home in a North African village is ransacked by Arabs, his wife dies and leaves him with a small child. Moving to Europe, he is able to regain his material wealth, but discovers that his daughter is blind and beyond medical help. An unexpected ray of light vanishes quickly, to leave utter darkness behind—Ditha miraculously gains her sight by a lightning-bolt, only to lose it soon afterwards by the same natural phenomenon. The place that was to become an oasis of peace reverts to the desert again from which this wandering Abdias came. Has he deserved all this because he strives for material goods, or because even in his happier hours he nurses the desire to avenge himself cruelly on the Arabs? His fate cannot be explained rationally. Walter Silz ranges the story among those that betray the other side of Stifter's serenity: 'Optimism about life may be Stifter's wish, but pessimism is his conviction.'

If this is true, then he had a remarkable ability to hide his innermost nature and make most of his works a revelation of peace and happiness. A disappointed lover contemplating murder in *Der beschriebene Tännling* is brought to his senses and back to a frugal, exemplary existence. In *Bergkristall* two children threatened by mountain snows are saved. The narrow-mindedness of the villagers, who regard all newcomers as unwelcome intruders, even the 'outsider' wife of one of their own number, resolves into harmonious integration, mainly as a result of the common anxiety felt about the two youngsters and of combined efforts to rescue them. In all these stories Stifter lets human nature, once it has reasserted its serenity, do the good work. There is no strained psychology. Persons of high and low status, but above all the villagers of Stifter's native Bohemia, can be led to accept the gentle law, without protest or loss of healthy vitality. The very language of these narratives, with their leisurely flow and pauses for detailed description, seems to remind us that it is only with unhurried pace that the benign designs of Providence can mature and reason and kindness be made to prevail.

All the claims of modesty notwithstanding, Stifter felt it incumbent on him to organize his ideas and ideals into a vast normative design of culture and history. In this case he admits that his effort is ambitious, and he hopes that posterity will recognize his achievement. The events of 1848 may have something to do with the conception of *Der Nachsommer* (1857). Stifter was shocked not so much by the demands of the revolutionaries as by their behaviour and by the threat of a transfer of power to classes not brought up in the heritage of Goethe and Schiller, or of Herder and Wilhelm von Humboldt. The *Nachsommer* seems to be one of those works that are destined to keep critics, even the well-disposed, for ever divided. For some it is a Utopia of propriety, harmony, love and friendship, to which a number of moneyed people can afford to retreat, thus avoiding contact with the harsher realities. Others, while admitting that as a novel the work exposes itself to such a negative interpretation, want the *Nachsommer* to be read as a defence of Platonism, or as an ethical message in allegorical dress, an exhortation to see in a happy family life—itself the result of individual perfection—the only guarantee for civilized progress.

Heinrich Drendorf, the son of a prosperous Viennese merchant, during one of the excursions that he undertakes as a student of nature and art, chances upon the 'Rosenhaus', whose owner, the nobleman von Risach, takes to him as a young man whom he would like to educate in the finest sense of the word. It is as if they had met by some pre-established harmony. Such harmonies are constantly at work among other arrivals at Risach's manor, notably between Heinrich and Natalie, and between Heinrich and Gustav, the children of Risach's friend Mathilde. At the end of the long novel, the engagement of Heinrich to Natalie is being celebrated in a ceremonial fashion resembling courtly ritual. With everything, from meals to tours through greenhouses, done in measured steps Stifter must have found it difficult to stage the engagement as a culminating solemnity. What reconciles us with these last pages, filled with stiff formalities, is Heinrich's resolve to go on studying and to pay greater attention to the natural sciences.

For with all the emphasis on conservation and preservation, on restoring old works of art rather than creating new ones, the *Nachsommer* takes into account that times are changing and technological interests increasing. Stifter welcomes the trend with the proviso, of course, that it will be made to serve man's needs or the ideals of Austrian humanity. And so the book can be read essentially as a preparation for the coming scientific and technical civilization, and for the spiritual forces that are to control it. Again Stifter is hopeful that this can be done. He inspires us with the feeling that Providence wants our happiness and has provided the love and goodwill, the reason and knowledge that are available to all human beings. Risach and Mathilde are themselves a source of love and wisdom for those around them, and the latter in turn, above all Heinrich, Natalie and Gustav, are living proof that young people feel instinctively drawn towards those who can enrich and ennoble their lives.

There are occasions when one might wish the younger generation to be less docile and to kick over the traces, as the heroes of other German educational novels are permitted to do. Stifter, if he antici-pated such a protest, countered it in the chapter *Rückblick*, Risach's story of his youth and the incident that separated him from Mathilde. As a tutor in her parental home he had fallen in love with the girl, but failed to rush to the parents and inform them of his emotions. When they learn about it they advise him to leave the house, and this he does, much to the consternation of Mathilde, who tells him to his face that he should have refused and fought for his love. Readers will jump to the same conclusion, only to be taught better. Passionate feelings must be subdued and submitted to the test of time. This is what Heinrich has to learn, while the other lesson, the right to revolt expressed by young Mathilde, is simply struck off the agenda—a measure of the supremacy of discipline over nature, or as some would have it, of theory over reality.

The *Nachsommer* is sealed off against other facets of reality as well; there is no place for the discussion of contemporary social and political problems. What then is the curriculum to which Heinrich and the other young people are subjected? Stifter arranges first of all for the proper kind of social intercourse. 'Erziehung ist wohl immer nur Umgang', we are told, and such basic virtues as dignity, reverence, and patience are the chief benefits derived from contact with the older generation. An unshakable belief in a benign universe is likewise imparted by teacher to student, as is the conviction that art is the foremost means for refining our emotions and clarifying our thoughts. Step by step word and action fall into line, to make life in the 'Rosenhaus' a paradigm of harmony and bliss. Risach even deems it necessary to help nature keep its biological equilibrium by providing the birds with insects and the insects with plants, without stopping to think that this balance exists only as a continuous life-and-death struggle. The psychological minefields to which Dostoevski's *Demons*, appearing in 1871, has led us are carefully circumvented by Stifter. The *Nachsommer* is in Max Rychner's view an intriguing display of all values created in the Western World, though it is a moonlit scene, ultimately receiving its light from Goethe.

The reproach that Stifter is unable to break out of Utopia to face the actualities of his time loses much of its validity when we go from the *Nachsommer* to *Witiko* (1865-67). It is well to remember that he worked on the two novels concurrently, on the one that cultivated 'Humanität' in the shelter of a wealthy aristocracy, and on the other that involved the same 'Humanität' in the turbulence of history, the rise of the Bohemian state in the twelfth century. If the *Nachsommer* was intended to prove that relations among civilized people can be refined to perfection by the gentle law and a reverence for cultural pursuits, *Witiko* is a demonstration, on a vast canvas, that nations can and must be built in harmony with the same spirit of humanity.

Witiko, the last scion of a noble family that has fallen on evil days, sets out on horseback from Passau in the direction of Bohemia. Adventurer or Parsifal? Rather the latter, a secularized presentation of the saintly knight, chosen by destiny to become the founder of Bohemia and its first ruler. Again, Providence is kindly disposed, and Witiko performs accordingly. He is at all times a gentle, humane warrior, a loyal lover and husband, a fatherly leader of his fellow-men from the Bohemian forests and a model for others who, when associated with him, fall under the spell of the gentle law. Even in war and bloodshed a restraining force is at work, and Stifter is careful enough to retouch some of the more brutal episodes by presenting the victors as good men, while defeat and death are the just reward for evil-doers. Yet he overstretches our patience when we have to accompany Witiko on expeditions with the German emperor against the Italians, punitive wars under the guise of restoring order. Here we have our doubts, while Witiko on his home ground, concerned with the foundation of a sort of welfare state for simple people, looks convincing as a statesman who performs political miracles by the magic of his humane thoughts and actions.

Witiko is not a novel based on history, it is a work which makes history plausible as a humane process. The assumption is a pre-established harmony between the vision of a wise, kind leader and the innermost yearnings of the masses of subjects. Stifter's persuasiveness in making us believe that early Bohemian history was enacted in the ideal, Platonic sense induces Eric Blackall to say that '*Witiko* is the only novel in German literature which is artistically satisfying;' and he finds that 'the only basis of comparison would be with Homer, Dante or the closing scenes of the *Nibelungenlied*.' It is not surprising that an Austrian should have attained such heights. The understanding of historical processes was native to Austrians, as was their insistence on tolerance and co-operation. They made, after all, the greatest effort in modern history, apart from the architects of the British Empire, to pacify a vast area embracing diverse nations. Grillparzer's Rudolf von Habsburg and Stifter's Witiko are spokesmen for the same hope, and while the one proclaims the kingdom of God on earth to be near, the other tries to show the feasibility of creating an ideal nation with the material at hand, to present men and women who want to live in peace and enjoy life in modest fashion. To believe in such a miracle one must be able to draw strength from the nature of man—and Austrian literature has, of course, tried hard to sketch an image of man which can supply such a humane conviction.

The war of 1866, severing Austria from Germany, did not alter the character of the Austrian cultural tradition. If anything, it tended to make Austria more conscious of regional traits and to underscore, now that the country was thrown back on its own resources, the missionary features of Austrian humanism.

Gifted writers were not lacking. Some were minor ones like Eduard von Bauernfeld (1802–90), a prolific producer of plays, narratives, and critical essays combining formal skill and didactic fervour, and Friedrich Halm (1806–71), whose one-time popularity as a dramatist has now shrunk to a respectful appreciation of his advanced realistic psychology. Others were major writers like

Marie von Ebner-Eschenbach (1830–1916), Ferdinand von Saar (1833–1906), Ludwig Anzengruber (1839–89), and Peter Rosegger (1843–1918). Anzengruber, the greatest of the lot, made both drama and novel a powerful means for discussing contemporary issues. The dramatic plot is usually suggested by an urgent social problem. The hero of his first play, *Der Pfarrer von Kirchfeld* (1870), is a priest who takes his calling seriously and thereby runs the risk of being reprimanded as a liberal or even as a free-thinker. This challenge to a lethargic church hierarchy came at a time when public opinion was agitated and divided by the recently proclaimed infallibility of the Pope. Almost all of Anzengruber's plays dare such direct reference to social and political questions. *Der Meineidbauer* (1872) is a stark tragedy not unworthy of comparison with Shakespeare's *Richard III*, while in the *Kreuzelschreiber* (1872), a comedy about an attempted marital strike of farmers' wives, instigated by an unscrupulous clergy in order to counter the men's opposition to a reactionary theology, we detect echoes of Aristophanes. *Das vierte Gebot* (1878), a gripping portrayal of improperly brought up children drew moving words of approval from Theodor Fontane. In all these works a terse dramatic style makes the pleas for a life of reason and kindness truly effective. Anzengruber's two novels *Der Schandfleck* (1877) and *Der Sternsteinhof* (1885) belong in the main stream of Austrian literature as well as to peasant writing. What a writer with only marginal experience of country life can do to simulate a peasant milieu Anzengruber has done with distinction, and as a preacher and moralist he is not inferior to Gotthelf. Rosegger, who limited himself to fiction but extended his interests to a variety of cultural aspects, has been dealt with in the context of peasant literature.

Marie von Ebner-Eschenbach was by birth and upbringing qualified to chronicle the life of the aristocracy—this would have been the first such record in Austrian literature. Many of her stories do indeed deal with the upper classes, mainly, however, to reproach them for neglect of their social obligations towards the lower classes. Her humanism, which springs from a warm heart and a lucid mind, shapes itself into a kind of voluntary socialism to be practised by the wealthy. She seems to be concerned in *Unsühnbar* (1890) with the then topical theme of adultery, but we soon find her veering in a different direction. While not condoning adultery, she inclines to relegate such transgressions to a minor role and to make the mutual devotion of husband and wife to the improvement of social conditions the purpose and binding power of marriage. Against Nietzsche she defends 'Mitleid' as our most valuable emotion, and, sceptical of radical cures, she demonstrates, in one of her best stories, *Der Kreisphysikus* in *Dorf- und Schlossgeschichten* (1883), the greater power of a feeling heart and a helping hand.

In depth of sympathy and in her courage in speaking for the underprivileged Marie von Ebner-Eschenbach stands in the forefront of socialist writing. *Er lasst die Hand küssen* (1886) is a shocking and brilliant exposure of an aristocracy despicable in its snobbery and cruelty to servants. She does not, however, fall into the error of idealizing her lower-class protégés. *Das Gemeindekind* (1887), a novel about a neglected country lad, whose father was a murderer and whose mother—though innocent—is in prison, reveals a general apathy towards a social outcast, even among the poor; happily, there appears also one of those truly humane characters who, like the heroes of *Oversberg* (1891) and *Rittmeister Brand* (1894), devote their lives to helping less fortunate fellow-beings. This favourite figure in Austrian literature, the good Samaritan who is also a full-blooded and joyful citizen of the world, remains an unforgettable character in Marie von Ebner-Eschenbach's narratives. With so much insistence placed on man as being naturally compassionate she subjects the artist to the test of social solidarity. Selfishness as a prerequisite to creative individualism finds no favour with her and is sternly rebuked in *Lotti, die Uhrmacherin* (1879), and in *Verschollen* (1896). If she is not sanguine about the support to be gleaned from art and artists in the social battle, she sets great store on men and women of innate or acquired kindliness, or on people who obey a sensitive conscience like the priest Leo in *Glaubenslos* (1893), who develops into a prototype of a worker's priest. Marie von Ebner-Eschenbach fulfils in creative expression the hopes which Bettina von Arnim had raised in her rhapsodic and semi-philosophical manifesto. In this and other respects the Austrian authoress is much superior to her German friend Louise von François (1817–93), who with all her pretended concern for the lower classes stays conservative in voicing her protest, basically convinced that a lax morality lies at the root of most social ills. Her novel *Die letzte Reckenburgerin* (1871) shows her to possess considerable narrative talent.

Ferdinand von Saar (1833–1906) comes as the last great Austrian writer whose creative span falls preponderantly into the nineteenth century. It is understandable that a mood of decadence was read into his writings, for some of them exude a feeling of resignation and ebbing vitality. He is fond of looking back on unhappy loves, as in *Requiem der Liebe* (1897), or on a promising career not completed, as in *Die Geigerin* (1875) and *Vae victis* (1879). Elegiac overtones, an excessively cultivated diction and a coolly analytical psychology appear to usher in an era in which aesthetic over-refinement combined with a lack of strong convictions. But this is only one aspect of Saar's work. Old skins were falling off, but underneath new ones were growing, nourished by a desire to be more realistic than traditional modes of description had allowed. This entailed among other things a more objective examination of the conditions in which servants and workers were living. *Die Steinklopfer* (1874) echoes to the hammer blows and dynamite explosions of the construction of the Semmering railway and looks closely at the workers and their plight. *Die Troglodytin* (1889) explores with the same almost naturalistic means the rural milieu and the tragedy of an outcast girl. But whatever the future was to bring—*fin de siècle* impressionism, the directness of naturalism, expressionism writhing with pain over the state of the world—the basic ingredients of the Austrian tradition and the style of clarity, serenity and understatement appropriate to them, were to reaffirm themselves time and again, even at the end of the First and Second World Wars.

8   *Bourgeois Literature*

The rise of the German middle classes and the formation of a bourgeoisie is for the historian and the sociologist one of the realities of the nineteenth century. They will readily concede that the beginnings of this process go far back, to the eighteenth and even to the sixteenth century, but it was the gradual liberalization during and after the era of Napoleon which helped to consolidate the gains of previous times and provided a political and economic cohesion justifying the terms 'middle class', 'bourgeois', 'bürgerlich', at least as a working hypothesis. The insistence on increased political freedom stimulated individual thought and feeling. In the eyes of the historian the liberal bourgeoisie suffered its decisive defeat in 1848, when it failed to unify Germany and secure a democratic constitution. With the resolve, some twenty years later, to throw in its lot with the national state of Bismarck, the bourgeoisie is thought to have forfeited the chance of determining the course of German history. But if the historian writes off the middle classes as a policy-making force from that time on, the sociologist continues to find the bourgeois a most interesting member of society. The same applies to the historian of literature, for bourgeois literature came into its own only after 1848. The writers whom we regard as expounding the essence of bourgeois thinking may perhaps admit that the ideal vision of bourgeois life had suffered a set-back at the hands of political forces, but they do not acknowledge a refutation of the values engendered by the middle classes. For obvious reasons they show greater faith in the survival of their ideals than the proponents of peasant mythology can muster. The vision of bourgeois life is less attached to environment and occupation than that of peasant literature. This is not to say that all spokesmen of the 'Bürgertum' were able to transcend the limitations of class prejudice, but the best of them can be seen to bear out Goethe's *laudatio*:

Wer ist das würdigste Glied des Staats? Ein wackerer Bürger;
Unter jeglicher Form bleibt er der edelste Stoff.

If we are to treat the system of bourgeois thought and its realizations as a kind of mythology—in the restricted sense that we have stressed—we must again remember, as in the case of peasant mythology, or of Austrian humanism, that the boundaries are not fixed and that they bulge out into the adjacent territories of other mythologies, Marxism and socialism included. Again the hope of converging developments is raised, a harmony of aims on the higher levels of solidarity and peaceful existence. For a long period bourgeois writing seems to play the leading role in this process of humanizing society. The bourgeois artist shows himself less limited in the selection of motifs than does the peasant or socialist. He can propagate his beliefs outside as well as inside the confines of middle-class life, confident that the essence of his values will be found in any man of inherent decency—provided, of course, that he has sufficient breadth of vision and sympathy.

The literary presentation of the supposedly universal validity of bourgeois ethics is governed by the desire for comprehensibility, and coincides with the final maturing of realistic style and composition. Fritz Martini has written the most extensive account of German literature from 1848 to 1898 under the title *Deutsche Literatur im bürgerlichen Realismus*. Realism and bourgeois merge into one concept, and the latter is all but identical with the significant writing of that period. This development takes place within a time marked by poetic realism at the beginning—the term was given new emphasis by Otto Ludwig (1813–65)—and the semi-impressionistic style of Fontane and others at the end.

Notwithstanding the allegedly universal applicability of their scale of values, bourgeois writers often point with pride to a sturdy middle-class *milieu* as the richest source of exemplary living and thinking. They are happy to come from a background such as Gottfried Keller described with deep gratitude when he sketched the picture of his father in *Der grüne Heinrich*. Theodor Storm felt strong affinities especially with the merchants and tradesmen of his environment, and for Otto Ludwig the attraction of a bourgeois milieu was decisive enough to make him focus his interests on writing. W. H. McClain points out that undistinguished as Ludwig's first literary attempts are, they excel in the presentation of such rural life as he knew from experience. The awareness of a specific talent for realistic description may have prompted him to give up a career as a musician; and while we regret his growing concern with the theory of the poetic, we are indebted to him both for the scenes of village and small-town life he describes and for a craftsmanship that was pledged to rigorous aesthetic standards. In this he is no exception among the realists of the nineteenth century. Interest in the bourgeois world merges with a desire to create true art; the subject matter, new and significant as it is, is not allowed to displace the greatest care in technique and form. The purpose, as Ludwig defined it, was to endow characters and events, however real they appear, with universal significance. We are once more close to the classical aim of making the particular phenomenon illuminate the general. Ludwig's knowledge of the English novelists Scott, Dickens, and George Eliot made him covet their intimate contact with the realities of society, a contact which would then help him to arrive at some generally valid meanings. For meaning cannot be durable without a foundation in a concrete world. Ludwig can say that true art is 'Kunst, die wieder Natur wird'—the closest anticipation of the definition of naturalistic art by Arno Holz—but he also emphasizes an older characteristic of poetic realism, a verisimilitude stripped of all superfluous accidentals.

Ludwig did not in his first narrative attempts escape the pitfall of distilling situations to the point where they reveal nothing but the bare bones of symbols, a method that diminishes the liveliness of that otherwise charming small-town story, *Die Heiterethei* (1854). In 1856 appeared his *chef d'oeuvre*, *Zwischen Himmel und Erde*, as concentrated an account of middle-class life as any, with the family of a slater in the foreground. Once the hero of the story, Apollonius Nettenmair, has returned home from working as a travelling journeyman we never leave his town again and hardly catch a glimpse of its surroundings, not even from the vantage point of the roofer on the church steeple. Town life is self-sufficient, socially and morally; the ethical code of middle-class life claims absolute validity and tolerates no adjustments to changing times. The justification of this state of affairs lies in the ability to sustain an exemplary family life even under the most adverse conditions. There is in Ludwig's world no suggestion of a dialectic process which will and ought to make way for changes, in order to smooth the path of progress and to allow for overdue corrections. If anything Ludwig holds the reins of bourgeois morality much more tightly than is customary in bourgeois writing.

The particular motif is one that we encounter frequently—a black sheep turns up in a highly virtuous family; its economic basis and moral credit are severely battered but are restored by the effort of some other member of the family. With a razor-sharp psychological insight Ludwig makes two brothers, Fritz and Apollonius, both of them slaters, drift apart, with the wife of Fritz as the innocent cause and victim of the quarrel. Fritz has originally stolen her from his brother, by slandering him. Apollonius, by the code of his class, must suppress his feelings for Christiane and try to live in peace with his brother. In addition to this heavy burden Apollonius is also saddled with the task of saving the business from ruin. Inner tension and suspense of action reach a climax when Fritz tries to push his brother down from the church tower but plunges to death himself. With the villain removed and a never disrupted affection between Apollonius and Christiane revealed anew, a belated marriage and blissful compensation for past sufferings are made possible, and even such a strict man as old Father Nettenmair advises, nay, insists on, such a course. But Apollonius stubbornly decides to stay single, a friend and provider for the family of his brother, not more. Though he is only the innocent cause of the death of his brother, a would-be murderer, he cannot claim the reward of an accident; if he did, the accident would become his deed, something, Ludwig seems to insinuate, Apollonius must have wished for deep down in his mind. Here and in other incidents we are on the trail leading to psychoanalytical concepts—as when Apollonius, suffering from an undefined illness, the result of all he has endured, climbs the church tower in a stormy night, to extinguish, at the risk of his life, a fire that might engulf the whole town. His heroism releases a cathartic process which restores him to health and confidence. There is, however, more to this event; it makes Apollonius the idol of the whole population. No upright 'Bürger' who secretly dreams of ingratiating himself with his fellow-citizens has seen his hopes come true more fully. The wish to be respected by the community is a deep-seated ambition of people living in a tightly knit society. A good reputation is the stamp of approval from the unerring collective conscience.

Zwischen Himmel und Erde lifts a man of sincerity, probity, and kindness on to the pedestal of abiding esteem. Composed with dramatic skill, the story, in spite of many animated scenes, steadily revolves around the problem of ethical behaviour. But while Apollonius obviously enjoys a pre-arranged harmony between virtue and contentment, the same cannot be said of the unfortunate hero of Ludwig's one successful play, *Der Erbförster* (1853). This time strength of character stiffens into narrow, though respectable, bourgeois ideals; virtue, without the tolerance born of a sense of humour, becomes sterile and downright dangerous, and the play turns into a dryly recorded story of the needless tragedy of unbending character. This makes Ludwig's basic limitation painfully clear— he cannot remove his 'Bürger' from his stifling atmosphere and transpose him to a more open field of action.

Gustav Freytag (1816–95) tried to do just this. A year before *Zwischen Himmel und Erde* he brought out a voluminous novel, *Soll und Haben*, with the motto: 'Ich möchte das deutsche Volk da zeigen, wo es am tüchtigsten ist, bei der Arbeit.' This is not necessarily the most interesting place. Freytag interlards the working day of his sturdy Germans with all manner of adventures, first in the upper stratum of a degenerating nobility, and then on the lower level of a ruthless, criminal scramble for money. Somewhat of an intellectual, at any rate an aspirant at one time to a university career as a Germanist, later the editor of a well-known weekly liberal *Die Grenzboten*, he saw the middle class evolving an ideal form of existence, open to all who are willing to work hard and serve honestly, and the mainstay of an expanding Fatherland as the carrier of national ideas. His novel was to give a cross-section of this development. An honest country lad works his way into partnership in a thriving business, but not without some adventures in high society and politics. Freytag regarded himself as in competition with Dickens, at that time a widely read author in Germany, and strained his imagination to lead his hero through a vast section of contemporary life. His aim was twofold: to show that the existence of a businessman can be as poetic or romantic as any, and to point out the temptations that must be resisted—mainly the fascination of hob-nobbing with aristocrats and the lure of easy gains by dishonest means—in this instance regrettably illustrated by a sort of Jewish underworld. For good measure Anton, the hero of the novel, before settling down to marry the sister of his business associate, becomes involved in a border clash between 'uncivilized' Poles and the bearers of German culture. Yet vast as the panorama is, it lacks vivacity of invention, freshness of style and, worst of all, the finer touches of humanity. It comes as no surprise that Freytag's further efforts in fiction rank as 'Professorenromane', erudite but stale.

Two years after *Soll und Haben* appeared Stifter's *Nachsommer*. Its superior qualities as an educational novel stand out all the more in a comparison with Freytag's pedestrian work. But, as we have said, Stifter's school is a private, aristocratic establishment, open only to a carefully selected bourgeoisie. The needs of the middle classes, and their problems, called for another type of educational novel. Gottfried Keller's (1819–90) *Der grüne Heinrich* (1855) meets the requirements of bourgeois mythology in this respect. It is the most important prose work of the middle of the century, and in the estimation of some the best piece of fiction in German literature, as fresh in emotion, thought and imagination as it is in style. Undisputed as its immensely poetic character is, the theme bears with captivating immediacy on the problems of the middle classes.

It was, as Keller was proud of stressing, 'the call of a lively period that awakened me and determined the course of my interests.' The allusion is to the political fermentation in his home town and canton of Zürich, and to the rise of liberalism, a cause he espoused fervently. To make his engagement unequivocally clear he put down the painter's brush, his first ambition, and turned to the pen. The shift might have come in any case, but it was characteristic of him that it occurred under the pressure of social and political concerns, and while he soon realized that his literary gifts went beyond political poetry, he nevertheless kept his life and work attuned to public interests—his last work, the novel *Martin Salander* (1886) is as much saturated with apprehension about the future of liberalism as his first writings had been with exuberant optimism.

The influence of Jean Paul and Goethe, strong as it was on young Keller, could neither limit him to classical canons nor entice him into the nebulous sphere of romanticism, though he was, by deep affinities, responsive to both. *Der grüne Heinrich* is a largely autobiographical novel, and Keller made the revised edition of 1879

even more so, giving it a symbolic or at least a representative meaning which accorded with the development of his own life. The three
painters in the novel who provide most of the content of the second
part now all abandon their artistic careers to devote themselves to
practical tasks, one as a parliamentarian, another in business and the
third, the author's alter ego, as a clerk on the lower rungs of the civil
service ladder. The intent is clear: where a talent is not great enough
to promise distinction, it is best to stop wasting time and to do
something more useful—but even where such a promise exists the
artist must still find ways and means to be useful to society. We
could add that *Der grüne Heinrich* contains a suggestion that art, at
any rate painting, may have run its course for the time being and be
in need of a restorative pause. However, when Keller was working
on the revision, his own long literary career disproved such a pessimistic view—what he did not renounce was his conviction that in
our democratic times everybody's duty is first of all to his community and that the exercise of artistic talent must be made subservient to it. This is, of course, a debatable theory, much as it
honours Keller's sense of civic obligation. In his own life he found
an ingenious solution to the problem of divided loyalties. Returning from Berlin in 1856, after establishing himself as a novelist and
an accomplished narrator, with the first volume of *Die Leute von
Seldwyla* (1856), he accepted, after some years of an unsatisfactory
free-lance career, the post of 'Staatsschreiber' for the canton of
Zürich, thereby assuming the demanding duties of secretary to the
cantonal parliament and to its executive body. Having completed
sixteen years of faithful service with little time off for his creative
work, he felt he had discharged his self-imposed obligation to the
community and earned the right to leave his office, to write the
works that had been collecting in his mind. Yet his interests were
never far from political and social questions. Other writers of this
realistic period—Storm and Fontane for instance—had their creative
work run concurrently with some practical occupation, likewise
exemplifying the new nexus between art and life and practising,
each in his own way, the fundamental tenets of a philosophy of
bourgeois life. But it remained for Keller to give this ideal its fullest
expression; his involvement in politics was stronger than that of
most others, and he gave himself an almost excessively long time to

ponder the problems of philosophy, religion, and the democratic way of life, in order to satisfy his sense of responsibility to all three forces. Unhurriedly, albeit steadily, probing and maturing his thoughts on man's place in the world, he had the good fortune, when he stayed in Heidelberg from 1848 to 1849, to become acquainted with Ludwig Feuerbach (1804–72), the philosopher who boldly cut the ties between man and God and proclaimed an atheism in which man took over the responsibilities—outlined by Christian ethics—that had hitherto been regarded as imposed on man by a divine being. The difficulties of this transfer of responsibility and the ensuing liberalization and secularization of institutions were eased by Feuerbach's strong emphasis on love as the distinguishing feature and a prime obligation of men; *their* sympathy, not that of an undefinable God, will bring about social peace and happiness. What Keller had long felt and yearned to believe on the strength of fact and reason, namely that man has become of age and is able to do right, in private and political life, out of the resources of his heart and mind, all this was given by Feuerbach the dignity of systematic thought and supported philosophically against attacks from theology. Feuerbach emboldened left-wing Hegelians to proclaim man the centre of all thought-structures—it is he who creates God in his own image. Keller left Heidelberg with a more exalted, not to say poetic feeling of the beauty of the world and the ennobling responsibility placed on man. Feuerbach's atheism was not and could not remain an essential part in his 'Weltfrömmigkeit'—it shrank to a little insect embedded in golden amber. Keller gradually returned to the Goethean concept of respect and deference for what is inexplicable, and his faith in man was qualified by a sceptical watchfulness, though his innate gratitude for the miracle of being remained unimpaired. Most of the realists of the nineteenth century drifted away from traditional metaphysics, Christian or otherwise, but not all of them were successful in staving off, like Keller, resignation and indifference. With rare warmth and immediacy he exhales faith and joy in life; if some of this flow of sympathy dries up in his last work, it is not because he has fallen into the clutches of anguish and despair, but because he feels disappointed in the people to whom this beautiful world has been entrusted, or at any rate in the democrats who have frittered away their rights and responsibilities.

The first version of *Der grüne Heinrich* starts with the account of a young Swiss journeying to a German capital, to perfect himself in the art of painting. At a later stage we are given, from a manuscript he has with him, an autobiographical story of his childhood and formative years. The revised edition of 1879 recounts everything in chronological order and in the first person. Textual changes are equally significant, particularly the one affecting the ending. In the first version Heinrich comes home, disappointed professionally, and morally dejected because he has left his widowed mother for a very long time without news. As he enters his home-town he meets a funeral procession and learns that it is his mother, dead through worry, whom they are burying. Remorse and sorrow make the son the next victim. In the second version the feeling of guilt through neglect is only slightly alleviated, but the punishment remitted. As we mentioned before, Heinrich decides to enter the public service and lives, if not cheerfully, then at any rate dutifully, resigning all worldly aspirations, including that of marrying a woman he once loved and who also has returned, from America, to live for the service of the sick and poor.

First version or second version, there is no difference in the eagerness and ability of Heinrich Lee to touch life at many points and to draw its joys and sorrows into his consciousness, and no difference in the psychological penetration of childhood; the *milieu*, lower middle-class in a Swiss city, remains of course the same, as does the change to an unnamed art centre in Germany—the Munich where Keller had undergone some of his less exhilarating experiences while trying to establish himself as a painter. Heinrich's development, in spite of all the seemingly independent yet highly interesting episodes, can be abstracted from the two versions. There is the image of a father who is remembered as a self-reliant stone mason and builder, forging ahead in his trade but giving unstintedly of his time to societies for the betterment and education of tradesmen and artisans. Heinrich falls heir to these upright progressive attitudes, though the newly won freedom of the middle classes will in due time involve him in great problems.

There is first of all a sense of independence in religious traditions. He no longer claims his right to his father's pew, his own God being a spiritual force aglow with 'Weltlichkeit' and best served outside the established churches by a love of our fellow-men. The liberalization of the middle classes also entails the duty of choosing a vocation in accordance with our most promising talents. Heinrich's obstinacy in enforcing his will to become a painter against all sorts of advisers and against the misgivings of his mother shows the risks which sons of the middle classes are now courting. The precarious position of the artist in a democratic society has been discussed in another context—Keller also comments on the equivocal position of the civil servant in a democracy, and on the advantages of republican states over monarchies. But lest anyone should think that these are dry and academic topics it cannot be repeated often enough that the novel raises and drops such discussions in wave after wave of lively incident, to fill us with a deeply emotional and joyous participation in life. Love has its full share in it, plucking as it does the heart-strings of young Heinrich in two keys, worldly and spiritual. Also, his gregariousness makes for an abundance of episodes and reflections on himself and others. Notwithstanding all Heinrich's gifts and ambitions, we see, long before he does, that his strongest characteristic is his sociability. It is for good reason that this delight in joining others leads to his expulsion from school, on account of a rowdy demonstration he could not resist tagging along with, only to be shoved to the head and punished as a ringleader. The incident occurred in Keller's own youth, and though it gave him and his alter ego in the novel a unique chance to develop at a leisurely pace and in great freedom, he looked back on it all his life as an unpardonable miscarriage of justice—the state has no right to deprive a youngster of his education, since a good schooling is the first prerequisite for the citizen of a democracy. He could on occasion claim that the novel was written as an accusation against the authorities who had perpetrated a decapitation of the mind. This is all nonsense, but it shows that Keller was not willing to acquiesce in such wrongdoing, even if in his own case it had most likely helped him to become the poet and writer he was. But the novel is anything but a *pièce de thèse*; it is a panegyric on life in a free, self-reliant society, a source from which the reader can replenish his dwindling acceptance of life, his failing emotional sensitivity, or his atrophying sense of humour.

The preface to the first volume of *Die Leute von Seldwyla* serves as a kind of framework; the stories all refer to some imaginary town of markedly Swiss characteristics; its inhabitants love fun more than hard work, they are always engaged in some prank. The picture Keller outlines is rather sketchy and not necessarily elaborated on in the stories within the frame. Some of these tales are overtly didactic. To speak of the first volume: *Frau Regel Amrain und ihr Jüngster* portrays an ideal woman and mother, who, when her shiftless husband leaves her alone with a son, sees to it that the latter will avoid the pitfalls of undisciplined life. One of the lessons she drives home is that he must take an interest in public affairs and not shun his duties as a citizen and voter. Similarly, in *Pankraz der Schmoller*, a young lad given to sulking and abstaining from normal contact with his fellow-beings is forced to undergo a drastic cure; he returns from military service in India and North Africa with the resolve to continue with my 'ability to work and my solid way of life in my home country.'

The other three stories of the first volume are a measure of Keller's artistic range. There is the serene fairy-tale story of *Spiegel, das Kätzchen*, the tom-cat who sells his fat to the town sorcerer in return for being well fed until he has put on the desired weight, but who, after being restored to health by a sumptuous diet, has much more intelligent afterthoughts, and is sly enough to slip out of the contract—a tale moving smoothly as if on cat's paws, and a special delight for the Marxist ideologist who believes that only a well-fed person can think and act realistically. *Die drei gerechten Kammacher* is, on the other hand, a vitriolic satire. It tells of three soulless, self-righteous comb-makers, paragons of virtue in letter but not in spirit, and of their competition for the hand of a cunning spinster and for a steady job with the local comb-maker. Two of them perish cruelly in the process, but the hardest punishment is meted out to the one who has to marry the horrible—and now almost legendary— Züs Bünzlin, an unforgettable agglomerate of pedantry, meanness, and stupidity. *Romeo und Julia auf dem Dorfe* at once proved to be the most popular story of the collection, a place it has retained even with the most sophisticated readers. It is the account of two children driven out of the paradise of their youth, from the farms which their fathers lose when they start to quarrel with one another and exhaust their wealth in endless litigation. Sali and Vrenchen meet again when they are grown up, and become aware

E

of their mutual affection in an episode of touching sadness: they try to separate their irate fathers who are locked in a fight. Poor and without prospect of a future, they decide to have a happy day together, an excursion in the countryside, for them a dream world in which they are taken to be husband and wife. With their fine qualities they can easily live up to such an ideal—but when night comes it is time either to separate again, or to take to the hills with a mad procession of rootless outsiders and gypsies. Excited by love, music, and wine they choose death together, untying a boat laden with hay and celebrating their nuptials as it drifts down the river— and as morning comes two bodies glide into the water. Moved by the innocence and charm of the two youngsters one cannot help wondering whether there was no way out for them—a fresh start in life with the hope of a later marriage. But Keller wants us to feel that the children's constant awareness of the former reputation of their parents, of how happy they might have been but for the stubborness of their fathers, their inability, as well, to tear themselves away from the countryside to which they belong, and their lack of experience and advice, make it impossible for them to live in a world whose middle-class standards they accept, even as outcasts. The end is a 'Liebestod', a Dionysian immersion in love and death, a natural and guiltless surrender of individuation to the elements, long before Wagner, Nietzsche and Thomas Mann had given such mystic orgies their philosophical blessing.

The second volume of *Die Leute von Seldwyla* (1874) excels in the same expert narration and vital relevance to the problems of life. Honesty, truthfulness, social concern form the values which have to reassert themselves in a world where pretence, hypocrisy and conventionality are making ominous inroads. With events from past and present, a wide scale of moods, and a strikingly rich assortment of characters, Keller elicits, directly or by inference, the timeless validity of basic ethical tenets. Frequently the artisan is the prototype of the model citizen, stamped in the image of his father. His exemplary creations are men and women of tranquil, generous disposition who find the role of mentor, good Samaritan, and fighter for their own rights and those of others much more to their liking than heroic gestures. How gleefully Keller helps true valour, even where it is masked by deceptive external circumstances or by inner confusion, how little he hesitates to promote a socially inferior person to bourgeois standing, is shown in *Kleider machen Leute*. An itinerant tailor, through virtually no fault of his own, is taken to be a count in exile, dined and wined in a small Swiss town and finally welcomed as the fiancé of the daughter of an upper-class family. When one of the local burghers, a competitor for the affection of the girl, stages a cruel unmasking of the false nobleman, Keller arranges for events which dispose of the vile bourgeois suitor and leave the poor tailor at the side of his bride-to-be. He can justify such a course by revealing the inner qualities of the hapless man in his most humiliating hour. A near-tragedy ends in marriage and a prosperous family and business, though—inserting a note of caution against the materialistic propensities of the bourgeoisie—Keller makes the hero of the story adjust to type and become richer, but not wiser or kinder.

Freed from the onerous duties of his office, Keller was able to complete some half-finished stories and start new ones. Even as 'Staatsschreiber' he had published *Die sieben Legenden* (1872), a serene and tactful treatment of legendary Christian figures, spiced with grains of worldly wisdom. In 1878 appeared another cycle of stories, *Die Züricher Novellen*. In one of these, *Das Fähnlein der sieben Aufrechten*, we are shown seven upright citizens who exhibit, in addition to great patriotic fervour and devotion to the community, some all too human traits, but who reconcile their differences in a riot of confusion, fun, and exemplary democratic speeches, on the occasion of one of those national festivals—a shooting match in this case—which Keller was fond of visiting as a source of rejuvenating communal feeling. The difficulties are too cleverly invented and too smoothly overcome, the problems not significant enough, to make us accept this story as 'the only great political and democratic piece of German fiction'. It cannot rank with Stifter's attempt in *Witiko* to create a nation out of the spirit of 'Humanität', or with Raabe's *Gutmanns Reisen*, where a new Germany originates as the offspring of bourgeois common sense, integrity and serenity. Keller's seven artisans and entrepreneurs merely save their friendship in a crisis and help the son of one of them marry the daughter of another. The political message is mounted in the form of a speech which the young man, winner of the bride and the shooting competition, has to deliver. The thoughts Keller provides him with revolve around the much-vaunted definition of democratic life as 'friendship in freedom', and rise to the memorable admonition: 'Achte jedes Mannes Vaterland, aber das deinige liebe.' As always, Keller's thought is emotional thought, though it is grounded in wisely sifted experience. In such a festive mood as the end of the story evokes, with nothing but plain, upright patriots around, he is apt to move in a vicious circle and eulogize the characters he has carefully tailored to democratic measure. The same collection of tales fortunately goes beyond the middle classes, to demonstrate the validity of bourgeois ideals in other spheres as well. Salomon Landolt, the central figure in *Der Landvogt von Greifensee*, belonged to a privileged class in the *ancien régime* yet can nevertheless become the embodiment of such timeless values as intelligence, responsibility towards others, and justice tempered with mercy. A bachelor who in spite of many attempts failed to find a suitable wife, mostly because the one party or the other is too responsible a person to hide or take lightly some serious biological or moral flaw, Landolt has become reconciled to resignation without ceasing to be a highly useful member of society. On the occasion of a gathering of all the women he once thought of marrying—a 'Kongress alter Schätze'—we are told of the circumstances which in each case led to acquaintance and separation, and treated to a fine exhibition of how much happiness and courage there can be in life, even if not every wish has come true.

In *Das Sinngedicht* (1881) Keller organizes a more successful search for the right kind of wife. A young scientist begins to feel the strain of too much work and, more important, becomes aware of an incipient atrophy of his emotional and moral faculties. Playfully Keller starts him on his expedition, and by a highly artistic arrangement of stories within the story, told for entertainment and used at the same time as arguments between Reinhart and an attractive young woman, Lucie, the author helps both of them to agree finally on the qualities that make for a suitable partnership in marriage. The choice of the right mate is, of course, a decisive step in the attainment of a purposeful human existence. The examples given come from many parts of the world in bygone and present times, and the qualities that matter, honesty, loyalty, kindness, are found under black and white skins, and in all walks of life. Middle-class society is by no means the only provider of such values, much as these are in harmony with its fondest aspirations. It may be no accident that Switzerland, through Keller, contributed some of the loftiest concepts and finest presentations to bourgeois mythology. But it was at the same time important that the ideals enshrined in it should appear to be independent of geographical accident. It is a measure of the perfection of the *Sinngedicht* that it achieved just this—the group of people entertaining, instructing and exploring each other through the stories belong to the culture of German classicism, and with it they combine both Swiss democratic spirit and a social behaviour reminiscent of the best English tradition. The outcome of it all, the engagement of Reinhart and Lucie, seems to guarantee the maturing of the best human qualities. It is friendship or love in freedom, which comes as the climax of the educational process in this school of marriage, a freedom stemming from our ability to choose and act in accordance with what, advised by rational insight and the promptings of a kind heart, we regard to be humane and helpful for us as well as for our fellow-beings.

There can be no question, as National Socialist critics claimed, that with his last book, the novel *Martin Salander*, Keller renounced his faith in democracy and in man's serious aspirations to 'Humanität'. For when all is said that can be advanced against the abuse of democracy by ruthless party politicians, when all the office hunters are exposed as crooks and sent to prison, when Keller has aired all his misgivings about a society that had relaxed its moral energy, he proceeded to show his hope that young Salander, the son of Martin, would rekindle the fire of civic idealism and continue the work of enlightened civilization. If the National Socialists delighted in seeing Keller raking together all the distortions of democratic government, Georg Lukács took the novel to indicate that finally after the respite given by a successful revision of the Swiss constitution in 1848, capitalistic greed was beginning to choke Swiss freedom as it had long choked freedom in Germany, and that Keller was voicing his disillusionment. But we have young Salander to gainsay this interpretation of the novel, and we have Keller's intention to write an optimistic sequel to it. We are over-pessimistic if we assume that with *Martin Salander* Keller was back in the days of his countryman Heinrich Zschokke (1771–1848), the ceaseless fighter for an enlightened bourgeoisie and peasantry, who in his story *Abenteuer der Neujahrsnacht* (1818) castigated the disdain of the nobility for the lower classes, in the narrative *Das Goldmacherdorf* (1817) illustrated how a fervently democratic, moralistic school teacher succeeds in transforming an economically and spiritually decaying village into a model community, and in his periodicals *Der Schweizerbote* (1798–1837) and *Stunden der Andacht* (1809–16) propagated the virtues of tolerance, industry and solidarity. Keller does not have to go over the same ground again; he can, even in *Martin Salander*, take a liberal-democratic society for granted and merely correct some of its flaws, the result of private failings more than of structural fissures.

In the North of Germany it was Theodor Storm (1817–88) who made his prose works—some fifty novellas—the medium which reflected, judged, and idealized middle-class life. Into these stories he brought strong moral convictions and the experience of rich and varied contacts with Frisia and Schleswig-Holstein. An enforced exile from his native province from 1853 to 1864, due to the Danish occupation, did much to accentuate his longing for the places of his childhood and early manhood. A natural gift has secured him an honourable place in the tradition of both folk and lyrical poetry, as it has also lent poetry to his narrative style. Many of his stories are told in the form of reminiscences, a presentation that favours lyrical moods and forms. Some of the earliest novellas and sketches from the past, such as *Im Saal* (1849), *Immensee* (1848), and *Angelika* (1855), may suffer from too much emotional moisture, but the label 'writer of "Stimmungsnovellen" ' must be taken to be honorific rather than critical. There is no excessive sentimentality in his mature work, and the charge of too much inwardness is all but groundless. Storm's characters are almost invariably endowed with great sensitiveness, but they do not for that reason withdraw into some sheltered sanctuary. Like Keller, with whom he carried on a highly expert correspondence on the writer's craft, Storm is an observant admirer and a responsible guardian of middle-class ethics. In the best of cases, and especially in small towns, the bourgeoisie forms a sort of patrician élite—sturdy people who are independent of the money and influence of the rich landowners in their neighbourhood, as Storm says in the opening pages of *Hans und Heinz Kirch* (1881). To maintain their exemplary status they have to gain and retain their own self-respect even more urgently than the respect of their fellow-citizens. Fortunately the qualities needed to give a good account of themselves in their trades and professions are basically the same that are postulated by their consciences as ethical values; industry, honesty, probity in our daily affairs are but the more manifest aspect of inner worth.

To preserve this world or to give it its solid foundation, an essential prerequisite is again loyalty in love and marriage. Storm turns with obvious relish to this theme and its variations. In *Immensee* the lovers are kept apart by a mother who wants to see her daughter married off as fast and as well as possible. A later encounter, too late to correct the situation, makes both aware that they have missed real happiness, and they flutter about like wounded nightingales. *Auf dem Staatshof* (1858) deals with a woman who spurns the man she really loves, to marry one whose wealth, she expects, will prevent the ruin of her family—a decision which in Storm's ethical world is doomed to end in tragedy. Unlike Fontane Storm does not recognize class barriers. A scholar of peasant origin disregards and overcomes, in the story *Im Schloss* (1861), such conventional objections and proves that with true love and manly courage all will turn out well. There are a number of works, mostly set in times when aristocratic pride and arrogance were most pronounced, in which Storm laughs at and triumphs over class prejudices. Even when, as in *Zur Chronik von Grieshuus* (1884), a nobleman marrying into a lower class has to pay the price in status and material possessions, Storm tolerates no such remorse as Fontane was all too fond of predicting. By the same token we are led to assume, in *Aquis submersus* (1877), that all would have turned out well if a young woman of the aristocracy had been allowed to marry the man of her choice, a bourgeois artist, by whom she is with child. Instead, she is forced to marry a Protestant minister and to endure a joyless life. Yet a chance meeting with her painter-friend shows her real feelings: during a few moments of a happy reunion her boy—their boy—slips away and drowns: *Culpa patris aquis submersus*. There are, however, other reasons why people fail to achieve happiness. In *Auf der Universität* (1862) a girl of modest circumstances proves too weak for the temptations of the city and the perfunctory amours of the students, and ends her life just at a time when a young artisan, who had long loved her, is ready to come to her rescue.

Industry and honesty are expected to a degree which the bourgeois hero is not always able to meet. *Carston Curator* (1877) depicts a man who, though occupying a modest station in the life of his native town, is given an office of great trust, administering the estates of orphaned minors. Civic virtue personified, he has to witness the moral deterioration of his only son and accept it as a form of punishment for having married the wrong kind of wife, a pleasure-loving woman unwilling to accompany him on the narrow path to a respectable middle-class existence. In the above mentioned story *Hans und Heinz Kirch* good bourgeois traditions, which in this case promise an expanding shipping firm, are betrayed by a son who goes to sea, only to return broken in body and spirit. This time it is the rigid mind of an unbending father that has driven the son into revolt. When old Kirch comes to realize his mistake, it is too late to mend things, and all he can do is to cling to the Christian hope of a reconciliation in another world. This is a rare expectation in Storm. Normally he looks askance at a second chance in an after-life, for it is in the *hic et nunc* that man wishes to fulfil his destiny by balancing enjoyment of life with impeccable moral conduct. As a consequence, he is not averse to exciting the pulse of sensuous vitality to beat with a strength unfamiliar to the reserved people of the North and the stern Protestant guardians of their mores. *Renate* (1878), in reports purporting to come down to us from the early eighteenth century, describes the independence and defiance of a young village beauty supected of witchcraft. When even the parson comes under the spell of her attractions, Storm provides him with enough intelligence and good fortune to enjoy Renate's company and take his clerical duties lightly. The response to physical beauty is most appropriately associated with an artist, a sculptor, in *Psyche* (1875). Saving a girl from drowning, he goes back to his studio to work on a statue of Psyche; a sensuous experience has given birth to art, and art will now in turn enhance life—a chance reunion with the girl, in front of his statue, seals their bliss. Storm, with the optimism of one who trusts in man's reason, has no apprehension concerning the artist's ability to integrate with bourgeois life and to be a good husband as well. The problem is demonstrated in reverse in *Pole Poppenspäler* (1874). An artisan marries the daughter of an itinerant puppeteer and willingly puts up with some inconvenience, caused mainly by the fiasco of his father-in-law, when the latter tries to stage a come-back. Love, and the courage of an upright 'Bürger' und 'Handwerker', can risk contact with the alien world of artists. Elsewhere it is the artist who acquires the habits of middle-class existence or at any rate avoids giving offence to them. The central figure of *Ein stiller Musikant* (1875) looks like a relative of Grillparzer's 'poor fiddler'. The difference is partly that Storm's musician is an accomplished piano-teacher, though unsuccessful in the concert hall and therefore too timid to woo the woman he loves, partly that he does not soar into the higher spheres of his Austrian counterpart. He makes the best of his talents as a teacher and has the satisfaction of instructing the daughter of the woman he once loved. She is his star pupil and honours him by singing one of his compositions. Storm's artists, in keeping with the sound attitude of the realist, claim no exalted place in society, and if they happen to be women they may well end up as good wives and mothers.

The chronological order of most of Storm's novellas—a framework with a narrator contributing the story either from his own recollections, from those of others, or from a manuscript—is apt to push events and ideas back into the past; the themes tend to assume an air of remoteness, and it is often only by a special effort that the author brings them to bear on his own time. But he comes close to doing so in *Ein Doppelgänger* (1886), which describes the plight of the released prisoner trying in vain to rehabilitate himself, and in *Ein Bekenntnis* (1887), where a doctor commits a mercy-killing on his wife, only to discover that a cure has now been found. To expiate his crime, for this is how he regards his lack of reverence for the sanctity of life, the doctor spends the rest of his days as a medical missionary in Africa. We shall hear of other bourgeois writers whose fondest dream is of a life of humanitarian service, embraced if possible under no other pressure than that of a sensitive conscience.

Storm's last work, for many his best, *Der Schimmelreiter* (1888), takes us back into the past, to isolate and thereby to delineate all the more clearly a problem of general social import: in times of extreme stress even a democratic society may have to accept the will and wisdom of some superior person. At the end of the story Storm invokes Socrates, who was given a deadly poison, and Christ, whom they crucified. We may no longer perpetrate such crimes but we are still capable of doing a great injustice to a man like Hauke Haien, the hero of *Der Schimmelreiter*, by turning him into a shadowy spectre. Hauke, as a model member of a community, goes further than his fellow-beings want him to go. They approve his rise from a modest cottage in the marshes to become, by dint of hard work and superior intelligence, the right-hand man of the 'Deichgraf', the official responsible for keeping the dikes in order. They have nothing against Hauke's succeeding the 'Deichgraf' and marrying his daughter, but when he more or less forces them into building more dikes and reclaiming more land they begin to balk. With Hauke refusing to follow an old superstition and to have a live dog buried in the new dike to make it impregnable, the villagers all but stage a rebellion. By a strange twist Hauke and his wife and child, on a stormy night with the dikes threatening to break, are swallowed up in the raging waters—as if superstition were right, after all, and a living being had to be sacrificed. Storm is, of course not defending irrationalism. But he shows how tenaciously such beliefs survive and how they are frequently supported by the dark elements of nature. The final impression is one of chaos transformed into order, and of the benefit Hauke's work brings to his people for years to come. Not that his fellow-men are made to appear unreasonable and ungenerous; apart from one villain in the story they form as progressive a community as any. Here, much more than in *Faust*, we feel the elation of 'auf freiem Grund mit freiem Volke stehn', for it is truly the people who cherish and work for their freedom. They are serious in their enlightened social demands, even if on the last stretch, tired by the superhuman efforts demanded of them, they weaken in their allegiance. *Der Schimmelreiter* does not stress the tragic fate to which a lethargic community condemns the man of vision, but is rather an illustration of the complex relationship between individual and society, each of which has inalienable rights to defend. In the final analysis the story, superbly written and rich in dramatic situations, deals with the scope and limit of co-operation among public-spirited men and women.

A widely read author in his lifetime, never left out of the histories of German literature—though often praised for the wrong books and the wrong qualities—claimed by a devoted 'Gemeinde' to be accessible only to those who can appreciate a quaint, whimsical, and even eccentric world, Wilhelm Raabe (1831–1910) is now being presented as one of the major novelists of Germany. A new appreciation of the excellence of Raabe's novels, as well as of their content and their message, has played a welcome part in this upgrading. Barker Fairley, who has argued Raabe's modernity consistently and vigorously, sees him as far ahead of his generation in refinement of narrative style, anticipating Thomas Mann and William Faulkner, among others, and introducing techniques which were later used by Proust, Conrad, and Schnitzler.

In our context of the middle-class conscience unfolding as a system of normative beliefs and social visions, Raabe's work emerges as easily the most imaginative and comprehensive projection of bourgeois mythology. He loves exploring and enriching the world of the common people, he takes us closer to mankind than any other nineteenth-century writer, to display its values or its foibles—for if he idealizes he is also very critical, using his best characters as a measuring-stick for the others. Raabe speaks with a profound knowledge of men, and of what has been thought and said about them, but remains unshaken in his conviction that the rank and file of humanity will time and again reach the standard of exemplary conduct. He is more concerned with inspiration than with indoctrination; his relentless search for new configurations posing new problems may have something to do with his preference for teaching by paradigmatic action instead of moral prescription.

How Raabe's first novel, *Die Chronik der Sperlingsgasse* (1856), earned him the reputation, long unquestioned, of a wayward, sentimental and over-nostalgic writer is hard to understand, if we read it with the experience of modern fiction. Both the narrator, an old man by the name of Wachholder, and his diary revealing the contacts he has cultivated among the neighbours in his street are treated realistically, and the milieu is viewed intelligently and objectively. The fact that all the sorrow and sadness crowded into this microcosm of a world—though there is joy and comfort as well—is met with genuine sympathy and prompts an immediate desire to help inevitably stirs emotions rather than ideas. It is Raabe's avowed purpose to reinvigorate our capacity for feeling and resensitize our gift of wonder at the miracle and beauty of being. We are reminded of Immermann's endeavour to share his 'Gemütswunder' with his readers, and similar declarations of intent by Jean Paul come to mind. That Raabe should wish to strike emotional chords will not surprise us in a German writer, though the fear of it being done excessively may make us feel uneasy. But in spite of the strong emotional over-tone in some of his books, Raabe has successfully squared the German circle: he activates emotive powers without blocking the intellectual arteries. *Die Chronik* augurs well for Raabe's later works. If much of what happens affects the heart as much as the mind, it is mainly because a pressing material need, the sickness and death of a child, or the betrayal of a woman, are bound to stimulate warm-hearted reactions. Issues of a more general character, the persecu-tion of democrats, or the decision of so many hapless people to emigrate—life in the 'Sperlingsgasse' is open-minded enough to extend to such broad national concerns—are likewise handled with deep and compassionate understanding.

Raabe's development, after his first book, indicates a unique relationship between emotional and intellectual or philosophical responses. His ideas are not limited to a range determined early in his career, as is often the case with an emotional writer; they grow in variety and in originality. He tries all possible interpretations of life, quoting from others who come to his succour. Like Jean Paul he finds most of these thought-structures only partially adequate and sees himself thrown back on a reality which, unless we dismiss it as absurd or illusory, we can control and make livable by learning to know it, that is to say by realizing the nature of our obligations to-wards our fellow-men. But before the reader jumps to the conclu-sion that this means a regression to a few basic emotions like 'love of thy neighbour', friendship, sympathy, which have been evoked and extolled ad nauseam, it must be added that Raabe steadily moves away from any kind of simplicity, emotional or intellectual. Distrustful of the conventional emotional vocabulary, like any good writer, and even more distrustful of the customary labels of kind hearts, honest citizens, lovers of mankind, and benefactors of society, he subjects such terms to rigid tests. He seems to equip himself, or the characters of his stories, with a measure of clear-sighted scepticism, sarcasm and caution, in order to guard them from judging and act-ing sentimentally and prematurely. This is not done in an attempt to disprove the reality of kindness, generosity and love, but in order to let no one pretend to these values before they have been tempered by the practice of living and applying them.

Such hardening of the kindest characters into sinewy, unsentimental types is more in evidence in his later works than in those of the earlier and middle period. It is absent in *Der Hungerpastor* (1864), once Raabe's most celebrated novel. Here the best-intentioned persons incline to emotional and intellectual flabbiness. It is unfortunate that the work, still erroneously classed as an 'Erziehungsroman', should continue to figure as a representative achievement. The sentimental overweight of its hero is a fault which Raabe was careful not to repeat, and the suspicion of racial bias, to which he exposed himself, cannot fail to mar his image even for those who know that there was never the slightest recurrence of a like nature in the whole of Raabe's later works. To pair Hans Unwirrsch, the paragon of a small-town lower-class boy prospering in life, spiritually, of course, not materially, with a villain of Jewish descent, sly where the German is naïve, sensual but not pious, hell-bent on forging ahead instead of trusting God and his deputies on earth—this remains a blemish on Raabe's reputation, even if it was invented for reasons of Dickensian effect. The reverse—goodness in the Jew and malice in the Christian boy—would have been much more in accordance with Raabe's later temper, as it would have formed an excellent catalyst for the scorn and satire he could shower on thoughtless, arrogant pedlars of prejudice. But, as we have said, this is the only instance of a shockingly poor taste in Raabe's work, and we should for that reason be able to judge his other stories with the fairness they deserve.

Der Hungerpastor, Abu Telfan (1867), and *Der Schüdderump* (1870) are still referred to as a trilogy. But for a tenuous link inserted by Raabe and the unauthenticated opinion of a contemporary critic there is no evidence that the three novels were planned as a related sequence. What they share, together with *Die Leute aus dem Walde* (1863), is a much greater length than Raabe's later novels. In *Abu Telfan* he confesses, with a humour that begs to be taken seriously, to an ambitious work—evidently a book that was to make its impact by virtue of its intellectual content. He may have entertained the same hope for each of the other three novels—but they all disappoint us, as they must have disappointed the author. The great explosion did not come off, and we can see why. In a work published in 1857, *Ein Frühling*, Raabe ventures a prophecy which sounds more like a threat. Provoked by the abuse of a poverty-stricken working girl, he predicts another Flood, this time social revolution. Raabe is not frightened by the coming cataclysm, though he hopes that the spirit of the Lord will hover above the waters, that is to say that decency and kindness will prevail. In a later edition the ominous prophecy is deleted. Raabe has had second thoughts and wants the world to change in a less violent way. He decides against Marxist-socialist mythology in favour of bourgeois evolution—though he sometimes comes close to associating his idea of progress with that of non-violent socialism. We are thus led to believe that the four long novels following *Ein Frühling* show a change from revolution to evolution, preparing the way for a non-violent coming of better times, *Die Leute aus dem Walde* and *Der Hungerpastor* rely heavily on mystic religious forces released by an evasive old man of wisdom in the first novel, and by the nebulously portrayed parson Hans Unwirrsch in the second. Raabe must have felt the vagueness of these messengers of the spirit, and their ineffectiveness as social reformers. In *Abu Telfan* he tried other approaches, that of the critic shaking his contemporaries out of their lethargy, and of the prophet exhorting them to penitence and a change of heart. The stage is set accordingly. Leonhard Hagebucher, the son of a small-town couple, petty and conventional people, returns from an absence of years and with a different outlook on German civilization. He has learnt his lesson, mostly as a slave in Africa. But this, and the urge to act as a sort of ferment, is all he has brought back, and the parents are soon caught wishing he had stayed where he was. However, he also finds willing ears to listen to him, sympathizers with his ugly, critical mood. Some have a real grievance against society, while others join him for the sake of the expected fun and commotion. The plan is to rent a hall in the nearby 'Residenzstadt', where Leonhard is to give a series of lectures, the hammer-blows that will drive sense into flaccid minds and produce the sparks to start the action. Raabe the narrator is at his best in staging the coup; using the tricks of expert narration, a mood of high expectation is evoked, wishful thinking as well as stage-fright come to life. The speaker has feverishly collected facts to give strength to his arguments; from the way he looks he seems to be constantly though silently rehearsing his first thundering lecture. Well-meant but conflicting advice is offered by all sorts of people, suspense builds up on many sides, and the reader's imagination is a few jumps ahead of it all and anticipates in detail the shattering impact Hagebucher will make on the populace. With his elevation to a national figure so imminent, it is not surprising that he attracts the attention of women and falls in love with a girl who will accompany him on his arduous path of social regeneration. Better still, Raabe relates in delightful fashion how the bombshell tossed into the audience explodes with the promised effect. Faces grow white or red, restlessness and consternation mount; to the immense satisfaction of Hagebucher's accomplices the speech is understood for what it was intended to be, a gauntlet hurled into the smug countenance of German and European civilization. There is only one fly in the ointment. Raabe can describe the visual events to perfection, but all his skill is needed to camouflage the fact that he cannot write a speech for his hero. He does not tell us what was said. We have to take the author's word for the effectiveness of Hagebucher's oratory, but are left in the dark about what his ideas are. We are supposed to be convinced and moved by a world-shaking message, a stern reckoning with our way of life, but much as we strain our ears, we do not hear the speaker. No one could have surpassed Raabe in the *mise en scène* of the lecture. But there was, at that time, only one man who could have acted as a ghost-writer and composed Hagebucher's speech: Friedrich Nietzsche.

This is not to cast doubt on Raabe as a thinker and a critic of culture. His comments in this area are as frequent as they are astute. Strung together in essay or aphoristic form they would show him to be a conscientious observer of and a deeply concerned commentator on the ruinous trends in modern civilization. Coming as they do from the mouths of his characters these scattered comments have the authority of experience; they explain the thoughts and feelings of living men wanting to act as much as possible in the context of reason and progress. To say what he wants to say Raabe has to show man in his community and man driven by the urge to help, not be delivering harangues, but by actual social participation.

Abu Telfan, the inflammatory speech Raabe could not write, and the results he could not describe—they peter out in a story of revenge on an aristocratic seducer—must have taught him that his way of changing the world was not through the release of a violent flood, nor through the mystic-religious word or the mercilessly critical intellect.

The novel after *Abu Telfan*, *Der Schüdderump*, clearly looks for a retreat from loudly proclaimed programmes; and as if in resignation and irresolution Raabe hesitates to occupy the position which in his later works provides him with the strength to write with hope again. For in spite of the great kindness of some of his characters and notwithstanding their unselfish and courageous efforts, the victim they try to save is ultimately abandoned to a cruel fate. It is inconceivable that in Raabe's later works such faith and generosity, such intelligence and constant application to the work of rescue, would have failed so completely as they do in *Der Schüdderump*, where *la canaille* has its way. The girl who is saved from the poor-house in which her unwed mother dies later cannot be snatched from the clutches of her brutal grandfather, a barber who, corruption personified, has become a war-profiteer and now wants his attractive granddaughter as a pawn in one of his deals. The forces of goodwill and practical Christianity—drawn largely from Fénelon, a source which Jean Paul was so fond of tapping—are doomed to helplessness. No wonder that the influence of Schopenhauer was taken to be an incontestable element in *Der Schüdderump*.

But if Raabe here accepted counsel—though not comfort—from the philosopher who stated the aimlessness of life and the blindness of all our planning, the next work he wrote is a complete recovery from such pessimism and embraces life exuberantly, in the wake of Schillerean idealism. Barker Fairley discovered in *Der Dräumling* (1872) an aesthetic manifesto to which Raabe from now on adheres. He invokes 'the goddess of things all at once', 'die Göttin des Durcheinander', and while he pretends that his plea remained unheard and that he had to continue obeying the 'brave, altverständige nüchterne Muse des Nacheinander', the novel leaves no doubt that he managed superbly to telescope events while making his intention completely lucid. It is easy to see that, beginning with *Der Dräumling*, Raabe has reached the level of consummate craftsmanship, and moves now from one masterpiece to another. If the odd work falls below our expectations this has nothing to do with the chronology of development. From the *Dräumling* on he practises that form of narration which establishes his modernity. There appear in his works a surprising number of intimate links between form and content; 'Durcheinander', the turbulent convergence of many events in one last riotous whirl of happenings, collision and *dénouement* at the same time, is practised in ever new variations. Other technical experiments are evident—what it all amounts to is that the last word, the final hint for the interpreter, is given by the form of Raabe's narration. The meaning is never wholly comprehensible without close attention to formal elements. Plurality of narrators is used with surprising effect, but what is more of a novelty is the presence, in many of his works, of a listener who listens for us, or makes us listen with heightened attention. Raabe involves us in the lives of his characters as no other nineteenth-century writer succeeded in doing. Like Storm and Keller he now and then tells a story within a story. But it is in most cases impossible to separate the two or to cast away the framing action—as we often feel tempted to do with Storm— and go on with the main story.

Der Dräumling does not introduce these technical features all at once; they appear where the story can best use them. Looking back to Raabe's first work, *Die Chronik der Sperlingsgasse*, we notice that he was even then in possession of a narrative skill which presaged his later excellence. Moreover, the richer narrative life Barker Fairley sensed in the very form of *Der Dräumling* is paralleled and confirmed by a spiritual upsurge. In this regard too we are closer to Raabe's earliest works than to his so-called trilogy. Raabe has regained his faith in man, and he bears witness to this by a serene mood and an inspired imagination. The events of the story result from the suggestion, dropped into a sleepy German 'Kleinstadt', to commemorate in 1859 the hundredth anniversary of Schiller's birth. Raabe could have made it 1849 and provided an even better reason to celebrate. But with all his deep appreciation of Goethe, it was Schiller he needed to invigorate public life and to evoke a spiritual atmosphere with which he must have felt in close accord; enthusiasm for a goal that lifts us out of our ruts, and at the same time touches the hearts and minds of all good common people. The plot in *Der Dräumling* carries, on the waves of lofty thoughts and emotions, a struggling painter and the girl he loves into the heaven of

F

marriage, past protesting class-conscious relatives and a wealthy but philistine rival. Raabe feels closer to Schiller than is commonly assumed. There is in him a strong moral bias; with all his power to entertain and his gift for captivating aesthetic sensibilities he is always on the war-path against lethargy of the heart and narrowness of the mind—and like Schiller he takes delight in the dramatic confrontation of his protagonists, bringing them face to face, and making them fight out the issues. We can assume that Raabe adhered to a philosophy of free will; yet his psychology is one of understanding and forgiveness. But he is not prepared to condone meanness. He never again reverts to the black-and-white design so deplorably practised in *Der Hungerpastor*, though strong contrasts prevail, and the difference between good and evil is not allowed to become blurred. If Schiller's characters speak with resounding pathos, Raabe's act with tenacity; they do not offer 'diesen Kuss der ganzen Welt', but dispense their goodwill in measured doses prescribed by love and intelligence. It is possible that Schiller's optimism was in essence transcendental, while Raabe's was of this world, a frame of reference within which life seems worth living, and the uncertainty of history and of unknown metaphysical aspects bearable. We sometimes have the impression that all he wants to do is to find some staunch human beings to help within limited precincts to correct the ravages of history, to offset the insouciance of the universe, and to keep the obtuseness of mankind in check. But even this, we shall see, is disproved by some works which set their aim higher—*Gutmanns Reisen* and *Unruhige Gäste;* the one boldly entrusts the fate of a whole nation to men of goodwill who can alleviate to some extent the horrors of history, while the other attempts to anchor individual life in timeless values, in an absolute devotion to suffering men.

With *Der Dräumling* Raabe has completed his apprenticeship. Our discussion of a few of his later works is intended to convey an idea of the dimensions he was now able to give to the myth of the good citizen.

From a group of tales and novels which mobilize the impulse of generosity against lethargy of mind and heart we single out the following: *Horacker* (1876), *Das Horn von Wanza* (1881), *Im alten Eisen* (1887), and *Stopfkuchen* (1891). They must at the same time be counted among Raabe's formally most exquisite creations. In the first named *Fama* sweeps into a small town, to tell how young Horacker has broken out of a detention home and is now cutting a murderous swath through society. Horacker, the son of poor villagers, has as a matter of fact simply walked out because he was yearning for his mother and his sweetheart. Two high-school teachers, Eckerbusch and Windwebel, the latter also an artist, happen to be on the way to visit a friend, Pastor Winckler, in the nearby village of Gansewinckel. Galloping rumour has it that the two have crossed the path of Horacker in the forest and been murdered by him. True, they have met the boy, but only to coax him to act reasonably, go along with them, and trust their efforts at arbitration between him and the authorities. Meanwhile Eckerbusch's wife has heard of the murder of her husband. Resolute and sceptical, she hires a coach to take her to Gansewinckel, forcing a colleague of her husband, a timid intellectual shaking in his boots, to accompany her. From another direction the district attorney is proceeding to the same place, to deal with the escapee. Raabe stages a brilliant display of converging movements on to the same scene, superbly timed, first entangling and then disentangling the threads of the plot. With the aid of the pastor and his admirable wife, Windwebel and Eckerbusch redeem their promise in the face of a final threat from an irate and stupid mob of villagers. Horacker will be dealt with neither cruelly nor sentimentally, but with good sense and kindness. All ends well for the time being, and until the ugly heads of ill-will and complacency rise again, here or somewhere else. Though Eckerbusch, the *spiritus rector* who with the Wincklers averts a near-tragedy and combats darkness with the light of intelligence, is referred to as 'the last corrector', this is not a symbolic allusion to a vanishing species of character. There are others like him who appear in Raabe's world. Thus in *Das Horn von Wanza* the interest a young nobleman takes in a poor lad and the friendship he extends to him result in Wanza's having a night-watchman who, perched high up in a tree, is a source of strength and wisdom to his community, as he is also the hub of a delightful round of activity. A basement second-hand shop in *Im alten Eisen* is a similar centre of humanity. Chance brings the proprietress Wendeline Cruse together with Peter Uhusen, an old friend. Both have in former years, as members of a theatrical company, travelled through the Old and New World and steeled their souls for the test they now face. They hear of the death of an old childhood friend and the plight in which she left her two orphaned children. Peter and Wendeline employ all possible stratagems to counter the cruelty of life and manage to provide for the future of the children. The inherent softness of these mature people can be guessed from their actions, though everything is done in a matter-of-fact way. It is a case of the diamond in the rough, drawn with humour. As always, such coping with a crisis serves as a touchstone, discovering and attracting some helpful people, one of them a prostitute, and exposing and repelling others, none with greater irony than an old school chum of Peter and Wendeline, the hollow aesthete and social climber Dr. Brokenkorb. While Raabe is free of class prejudice, he can be savagely sarcastic towards an educated verbosity that lacks the sinews of conviction and corresponding action.

Stopfkuchen is one more such near-perfect creation of the artist and mentor of humanity. It is possible to lose oneself in admiration either of content or of form, yet each speaks for the depth of Raabe's mind. Heinrich Schaumann, the hero of this 'See- und Mordgeschichte', as the subtitle reads—it is an additional treat to see it verified in the end—has three strikes against him, even in the eyes of broad-minded people. He is a born anti-hero. His gluttonous taste for a special kind of pie makes him both fat and ridiculous, earning him the nickname of 'the sloth'—no wonder that he becomes a drop-out, if not in high-school, then at the university. Parents and teachers, friends and townspeople, all overlook his one redeeming quality which we the readers of his story are quick to discover: there is a greater promise of humanity in him than in all the others. He is loyal in his affections though they mark him as a non-conformist and make him even more of an outcast. He forms a deep attachment to another misfit, the daughter of Quakatz, who farms on what is called the 'Red Redoubt'; the place, used as a rampart in the Seven Years' War, now serves in the private war between Quakatz and his surrounding world. For the farmer has lived in the shadow of suspicion of murder since the day a wealthy cattle-dealer was found slain on the highway. Quakatz, to anticipate, is innocent, though by no means undeserving of some discomfort, grouchy and uncommunicative as he is. The case is still being widely discussed when Heinrich, chased by his classmates, bursts into the bastion, bleeding and with his clothes torn. He has found a place to live in, and a life to give meaning to, first by loving and marrying the daughter of Quakatz, and then by discovering and revealing the true murderer, though at his own leisurely pace. For when he finally obtains from an old country postman the confession of how he killed the arrogant cattle-dealer, driven by extreme provocation, Heinrich witholds his knowledge until after the death of the guilty man. He takes the law into his own hands, an extraordinary privilege which Raabe arrogates to himself—or to Heinrich Schaumann—as an exception that must be made on occasion, though it can only be made by a man of such rare independence of mind as Heinrich has. When the time comes, he goes to the village inn, where he hasn't been for years, to release the startling news to a friend who has come to visit him from Africa, and indirectly also to the waitress serving them. The town soon shares his revelation, while Heinrich returns to his redoubt and his wife.

Heinrich Schaumann is no rebel against existing law and order, much as he has had cause to avenge himself on a society that regarded him as expendable. But he lands squarely on his feet, and as if by an act of destiny he can go on developing into a man of extraordinary 'Souveränität'. For once, Raabe goes out of his way to grant an individual, who seems to shun all contacts with his fellow-beings, the right to live and think all by himself, with only his wife to keep him company. But this unique situation never leads to truculence, it is not stressed, and only the form of the novel and its unique framework make us aware of it. These however leave no doubt that Heinrich is meant to occupy the centre of the stage. The story of his life and the detective episode that is part of it are described by an old schoolmate of his, Eduard by name, who is now on his way back to South Africa. The very fact that he tells us next to nothing of his own experiences, though it is hinted that they must be of considerable interest, helps to raise Schaumann to an isolated and exalted position. While Eduard is travelling around half the globe we are naturally cognizant of the vast expanse of the world; and to feel the even greater dimensions of the universe there are always the stars to make them visibly lucent. As Eduard writes down the one noteworthy recollection he has gathered in Europe, we come back continually from these observations to Heinrich Schaumann. He himself, in turn, evokes historical reminiscences that come naturally from one who lives on an old rampart. The threads of time extend down into prehistory; Heinrich, a respected amateur palaeontologist, ties them to the beginning of planetary life—yet all the while we never lose sight of his unobtrusively suggested central place.

While it can be argued that most of Raabe's works—in addition to those mentioned there are *Hastenbeck* (1898), *Das Odfeld* (1887), *Kloster Lugau* (1893), and many others—revolve around a courageous and humane individual, there are a few which deal with more general aspects of the cultural, political, and religious problems that weighed upon the minds of his contemporaries. *Pfisters Mühle* (1884) is a richly modulated though not quite convincing attempt to ease, for the man of sentiment and classical learning, the transition from an allegedly cultured rural life to existence in a growing industrial civilization. Raabe's humour, usually a means of reconciling contrasts and disharmonies, is here used as a flimsily constructed bridge over which the flag of old-time values may be carried to a technological world, a chemical laundry, in this case, run by a man who still reads his Greek and Latin authors. By comparison, the religious theme in *Unruhige Gäste* (1884) is handled in much greater depth, though more by an account of actual experience than by theoretical discussion. The question Raabe asks himself is how far we must push the demands of radical humanism or of pure Christian ethics. With a language and a mode of thought that owe something to Biblical sources Raabe draws a sharp line between the children of the world and those few others who are wholly devoted to the works of charity. The interesting point is that while the highest manifestation of *agape* is found in a woman trained as a nurse, we are given to understand that the same qualities can occur outside the frame of Christianity, in this case in a socialist—sometimes referred to as communist—of a most unselfish disposition. And, needless to say in view of Raabe's psychology, they can occur in a gruff and seemingly misanthropic outsider. In *Unruhige Gäste* one of the 'Kinder der Welt' seriously contemplates crossing the dividing line but has to admit defeat, without Raabe's taking him to account for it, knowing as he does how difficult it is to leave the grooves of comfortable

living, which can be decent living nevertheless. Are we to understand that Christianity—or idealistic communism—presents too hard
a task for most of us? This contention was made at the turn of the
century by writers who, inspired by Nietzsche, granted man the
right to a less constricted self and a freer reliance on the promptings
of natural instincts. The bourgeois world hesitated to make such
concessions, or at any rate to admit that the aims of Christian ethics
or social idealism had been set too high. Practical considerations
were not allowed to invalidate these ultimate aspirations. In his last
work, the fragment *Altershausen* (1899), Raabe tries once more to
convert a 'Kind der Welt' to the practice of *agape*—whether of the
Christian or socialistic observance is irrelevant.

Society, in order to be spiritually leavened, must be kept aware of
such transcendent values and of the paths leading to them. Nations
on the other hand can be built with less saintly material. This is the
demonstration we witness in *Gutmanns Reisen* (1891). Boldly Raabe
takes over the meeting of the 'Deutsche Nationalverein' at Koburg,
in 1862, which was to draft a liberal constitution, and turns it into
a successful unification of Germany—a new German 'Reich' is
established with no more force than is required to prise the delegates loose from their cosy homes and set them on the train to
Koburg. An assembly of upright citizens, a larger number of them
than Keller had mobilized in his *Fähnlein*, suffices to lay the foundation of a civilized nation, pledged to peace and 'Humanität'. Raabe
wants to convince us that the virtues of the middle classes are the
best ingredients for a sound country and that the concept of the new
German state can arise from no better quarter than from the merry
delegates at Koburg who are as much inspired by the idyllic and
romantic atmosphere at nearby Wunsiedel, Jean Paul's birthplace,
as they are by a civic idealism of classical provenience. History, as we
are only too well aware, has side-tracked the good intentions of
Raabe's nation-builders—wherever the blame belongs, we cannot
place it on them, nor on their creator Raabe or any other of the
bourgeois writers. *Gutmanns Reisen* does not, like *Witiko*, have to
retouch history to make it coterminous with humaneness; Raabe
pretends to give a realistic picture of political life, plausible even if it
was not borne out by the actual course of history. In comparison
with the Keller work just mentioned Raabe's political Utopia—for

this is what the novel became, against its own will—is much more ambitious; it ventures to create a whole nation in the image of middle-class hopes. Raabe lived long enough to see his vision wiped out by reality. But he did not retreat into pessimism. He held to the position which accorded with his innermost beliefs—that the best we can do is to help others as much as we can—*omnes quantum potes iuva*. Inner refinement is a prerequisite to such conduct.

Raabe's last message to this effect, the twenty-odd pages of *Altershausen*, speaks clearly enough. It is never too late for a complete change of heart, a change in the direction of absolute kindness. Professor Feyerabend is seventy years old when in the midst of his birthday festivities and a shower of honours bestowed on him he loses all taste for a life of prominence and decides to return to his native village. His experience there is such that he comes to crave a combination of two ways of life: to be as simple and yet receptive to the charm of rural surroundings as an old school friend of his, whose mental growth was arrested long ago, and to practise *agape* as does a woman who has looked after the idiot boy ever since he has needed help.

Theodor Fontane (1819–98) published his first novel, *Vor dem Sturm*, in 1878 and wrote his best works between 1880—or more exactly 1888—and the end of his life. The turbulent years around 1848 had their impact on his thinking and strengthened his liberal convictions, but he failed to respond creatively, as Keller had done, to the clarion call of social activism, and by the time he started chronicling the life of Berlin, and more particularly that of the aristocratic society of the Mark Brandenburg, he had reached the age of a detached observer of the human condition, with a great love of life in general and an ironic view of some of its facets. The ambitions of the middle classes had largely turned to satisfaction with material possessions. For refinement, a liberal education, and a mature outlook tempered by irony, one had to go to the weathered mansions of the landed gentry. Fontane realized that the aristocracy, in the coming reconstruction of society, would lose its political significance, but he had no intention of accelerating the process. In any case, he expected the lower classes rather than the bourgeoisie to inherit the relinquished power. The middle classes had gained most of the rights they had asked for in the second half of the century and were now succumbing to cultural obesity. It was up to the workers to express real grievances and demand greater rights. Fontane threw his support in with the socialists, in his mild-mannered way. For in the main he shows little partisan bias. His sceptical mind tolerated no sanguine hopes and fantastic schemes, and his practice of tolerance and patience applied to all spheres of life.

The positing of universal values seems to have been a tempting speculation for him as for other bourgeois writers who show little sign of feeling bound by ideological limits. There was much more leeway for them than Marxist philosophy, with its many theoretical task-masters, allowed for. In actual fact the bourgeois was defined *a posteriori*, and it is a moot question whether all the definitions given are not more a revelation of bias than of insight. The middle-class mythology, as developed by Keller, Raabe, Storm, Fontane and even by Freytag and Heyse, was less attached to economic factors than to the tradition of enlightenment and idealism. The convergence of its humanism with that of the Austrian tradition, as also with that of idealistic socialism, is not surprising, considering the common roots of thought in the philosophy of the eighteenth and nineteenth centuries. Some writers seem to have come to crossroads where only accident determined whether they took the turning to socialism or continued on the bourgeois route. Spielhagen travelled now in the one direction, now in the other, and Fontane at one time planned to write a novel on the 'Likedeelers', a group of early communists—he might well have continued on this road.

The relative ease with which Fontane, once he turned to fiction, produced a handful of masterpieces is partly explained by the fact that he had been a professional journalist before becoming a novelist, and that he had experimented with the ballad before turning to the genre that was to draw out his more specific gifts. Among these was, as we have said, an epic tranquillity of mind, an eye for the serene side of life, and genuine feeling for its tragic aspects. If he refrained as much as possible from stirring up radical agitation, he tried at the same time to offer assistance and advice—*fortiter in re, suaviter in modo*—and the suavity of his method must not deceive us as to the fortitude of his convictions. We have referred to the advanced years in which he wrote his novels, but his mellowness is not simply that of old age. His forebears, Huguenot *émigrés* from Gascony, may account for his preference for enjoying life rather than making it tensely intellectual. We are inclined to attach great importance to Fontane's years in England, first as a teacher of German and later as a correspondent for a Berlin newspaper. He was predisposed to like the social and intellectual climate of London, the basic liberalism and the insistence on pragmatic utility rather than on unattainable perfection, and the broad humanity that protects the rights of the individual. Some of Fontane's characters, novices in the school of humanism, are sent to England, for shorter or longer periods, though others may attain to the same mastery over pride, haughtiness and ostentation without ever setting foot in the British Isles, as if all countries and walks of life could be entrusted with the breeding of gentlemen.

Fontane's knowledge of English enabled him to appreciate Scott as a writer of historical novels. Yet his own attempt in this line, *Vor dem Sturm*, profits little from either Scott or his German counterpart on a lower level, Willibald Alexis (1798–1871), whose real name was Georg Wilhelm Heinrich Häring. Honoured with the title of 'the Scott of the Mark Brandenburg' Alexis covered in voluminous novels such as *Der Roland von Berlin* (1840), *Der falsche Woldemar* (1842), *Die Hosen des Herrn von Bredow* (1846), *Ruhe ist die erste Bürgerpflicht* (1852), and *Isegrimm* (1854), a great deal of North German history after 1815, with deftly drawn characters more often than not veering in the direction of a liberalism taken over from Young Germany. There was scope for the development of a more ambitious German historical novel, but Fontane was not the writer to fill the gap. In *Vor dem Sturm* he describes the first signs of open opposition to Napoleon, after his retreat from Russia, with an attack on the French garrison at Frankfurt on the Oder emerging as a concrete plan. In spite of this central event—an abortive expedition from which the participants have to beat a hasty and inglorious retreat—the novel remains a mosaic of episodes; it is precisely in these historical vignettes and in the character-portraits that Fontane's charm and skill become most evident. A reader starting with *Vor dem Sturm* will very likely approach Fontane's subsequent works with the hope that whatever the author may do to tighten the composition of his work, he will not sacrifice the anecdotal, the *causeries*, and the digressions from the beaten track of history, particularly into the life of the Mark Brandenburg. Throughout his career his *Wanderungen durch die Mark Brandenburg* (1862–82) served him as a storehouse of regional details.

Some of the deeper levels of Fontane's art are, however, also prefigured in his first novel. The ill-prepared expedition against the French is strangely in accord with Fontane's non-belligerent attitude. Rather than drive his soldiers into battle, with the bugles of heroism blowing, he takes command of characters who, with all their patriotism, remain human, trying to avoid bloodshed and refusing to kill a French sentry by stealth. Fontane is obviously relieved when he can call off the skirmish and arrange for a comical retreat; his heart is not in the fight, and perhaps not even as unequivocally on the German side as the historical situation asks for. During all the preparations for liberation from the French, respect for their culture remains undiminished and is openly voiced. In this and other ways the work reveals some general traits of Fontane and his novels. No hatred comes to life in any of his human creations. Fontane the narrator hardly ever turns against individuals; vehemently as he can speak out against institutions and particularly against the obnoxious qualities of certain groups of people, the individual, however mean, disarms him. When in *Der Stechlin* he proudly remarks that in the Mark Brandenburg no saints were beatified, but no witches burnt either, he pin-points his fondness for tolerance and reasonableness.

That his most bitter diatribes should be reserved for the bourgeoisie may come as a surprise. He does not, however, disparage his own milieu and mythology—what he dislikes is people who, within the liberties available for the politically uncommitted middle classes, pursue materialistic aims solely. Such specimens he found among the beneficiaries of the 'Gründerzeit', the boom period after 1870, eager upstarts who delighted the artist as much as they must have annoyed him as a moralist. On these ambitious types, who were wholly impervious to the values he cherished, or worse still, paid lip service to them, he heaped his sarcasm. At the height of his powers, and after he had dealt with such more specific problems as adultery in the upper middle class in *L'Adultera* (1882) and *Cécile* (1887), he wrote two novels that reflect his attitude to the objectionable characteristics of the bourgeoisie, as he saw them. *Mathilde Möhring* (1907 posthumously) is a *Stopfkuchen* in reverse. For this time the easy-going and good-natured hero is not allowed to follow his own inclinations. The daughter of his Berlin landlady takes matters in hand and sees to it that the student Grossmann falls in love with her, passes his exams and, after their marriage, keeps on a steady keel of professional and social ambition. The way in which she all but succeeds is told with the serene insight of one who knows the one-track mind of a calculating person like Mathilde, with sympathy for the victim, her husband, whose phlegm, if nothing else, resists her efforts, and with the delight, mixed with sadness, of an author who deplores the bourgeoisie's habit of abusing its hard-earned opportunities, and has his own way of thwarting unsavoury plans, in the case of *Mathilde Möhring* by removing the innocent victim from the scene of cunning female design. But then, as if to restore the balance of realistic presentation, he shows us the young widow accepting her fate bravely. She may not be richer in wisdom but her determination is unbroken, and so she steps down to a modest existence as a school teacher. Fontane, we sense, has nothing against the middle class from which Mathilde comes and in which she wants to rise, but everything against a life that becomes a mere balance-sheet of material success and social prestige. What he misses, of course, is not religious or metaphysical propensities, but a plain humanity that knows how to relax and watch the procession of thrusters pass by with amusement and contempt.

A more specific analysis of the objectionable qualities of bourgeois mentality is found in *Frau Jenny Treibel* (1892). This time Fontane has a number of people on whom he can practise his satirical criticism. Frau Treibel, the wife of a prosperous industrialist, was, as a young girl of modest background, the friend of a boy from the neighbourhood, Schmidt, and together they indulged in a great deal of poetic and idealistic talking. But she let the boy move on alone on the path to true education, to become a high-school teacher. For herself she preferred to look for a well-to-do husband such as Treibel. Fontane knows that not much could be said against such a choice, were it not for the fact that Mrs. Treibel is in the habit, whenever the occasion arises, of continuing her sham eulogies of poetry and 'Bildung', thus ridiculing a set of values which is as dear to the author as it is to Schmidt. Fontane arranges for the exposure of Mrs. Treibel when her son falls in love with Schmidt's daughter Corinna.

She pretends to have nothing but admiration for the cultured atmosphere in which Corinna has been brought up, but in reality she suspects the Schmidt household of a sinister design to associate with a rich family like her own. Resolutely she severs the bond forming between her son and Corinna. The result is far from tragic, and sad only for the Treibels, who miss absorbing some intelligence into their milieu, while Corinna, not one to love passionately and hanker for long after a mother's boy of questionable manliness, will marry a teacher, the friend of her father. She will be fully compensated intellectually and emotionally for the immature cravings that made her cultivate the Treibels, by her own admission as an easy way to a life of luxury. This correction made and the tribute to the materialistic temptation of the 'Gründerzeit' paid, Fontane seems to suggest, the middle classes can rise again to become the élite of cultured human beings. But not even Treibel himself is allowed to become that typical caricature of the bourgeois which was presented from then on by so many simplifiers in literature and art, the obese man with a big cigar in his mouth, whose dog eats a beefsteak while some poor suppliant is told to clear out and work harder.

We have mentioned that nineteenth century writers made gallant efforts to jump the hurdles of class differences or to plead with conviction for their removal. Fontane is not one of them.

Two of his novels, *Irrungen, Wirrungen* (1888) and *Stine* (1890), deal with such class conflicts. The latter was started years earlier, but then displaced by *Irrungen, Wirrungen*, whose plot, or the kind of treatment Fontane was going to give it, proved more attractive. Waldemar, the young count in *Stine* who falls in love with a seamstress, cannot be brought to his senses and dissuaded from crossing the dividing line between the classes. When his best friends try to reason him out of his plan, and the girl herself remains cool to it, he is driven to suicide. The conflict is as much between the two lovers as it is between them and society, and this can hardly have been Fontane's intention. But with *Irrungen, Wirrungen* in progress he could allow himself, in *Stine*, to indulge in milieu description. The reader has nothing to regret. One of Waldemar's uncles has a liaison with a gay and plucky widow by the name of Pittelkow, whom he visits from time to time in her modest flat in a Berlin tenement house. If he turns up with other men who are amorously inclined the widow calls in additional ladies. It is on such an occasion that Waldemar comes to meet Stine, and the two, instead of playing the game according to rules, form a deep attachment. The relationship of Mrs. Pittelkow with Count 'Sarastro' could not fail to stimulate Fontane's wit and irony, and he exploited them more freely than the structure of the novel called for. But the widow is not unworthy of comparison with Hauptmann's 'Mutter Wolffen' in *Der Biberpelz*, indulging the whims of her aristocratic roué without being servile, sinning against the code of conventional ethics but preserving virtues that rank high in Fontane's esteem. She has the vitality to enjoy the company of her baron, the strength of character to keep his vulgarity in check, and the intelligence to know her place in life. This is Berlin milieu description at its best, bringing into play Fontane's understanding and love of the common people, though it does not seriously set social antagonisms in motion.

Irrungen, Wirrungen was to redress the balance in perfect form. The love between a nobleman and a Berlin working girl, and its termination in the spirit of mutual affection controlled by insight into the necessity of resignation and by the resolve to be loyal to new partners is now fully developed and articulated with the finest nuances. The sphere of Mrs. Pittelkow and her more robust attachments is reduced to reminiscences of a subsidiary character, without too great a loss in humour and in realistic depiction of milieu. Lene, the girl who is willing to pay the cost for a happy summer with Baron Botho von Rienäcker, is a rare creation in German literature. She has the emotions to make love a blissful experience and the intelligence not to let vain hope rise. The possibility of marriage with Botho never enters her mind. It does however enter Botho's and it falls to him to reflect on the inadvisability of such a match and to follow Fontane's advice against it. The reasons are those of a man who distrusts and dislikes the heroic gestures of defying the barriers of convention and of forfeiting the privileges of a higher station in life. True enough, the girl Botho loves gives every assurance of lasting human qualities. But what could they hope for from marriage? A *déclassé* officer could not earn a living outside the pale of his protected existence and would either live to regret and reverse his decision or abide by it and feel misplaced. Life to be happy requires order, the contentment of filling the place assigned to us by an evolutionary social process, and if our feelings on occasion trespass into higher or lower strata reason should call them back, and leave the social order undisturbed. This does not preclude the slow change of the social structure, but Fontane does not press for it. Fundamentally his conservative attitude may issue from the reflection that the risks of stepping over into other social spheres are too great—entailing as they do the danger of not obtaining the expected happiness and of diminishing our chance to mature into serene, humane persons. The social and material gains accruing, perhaps, from a rise to a higher stratum are negligible in any case, and the squandering of the best human qualities would be disastrous to society. A sensible bourgeois mentality takes pride in its civic virtues and places them higher than the questionable advantage of social rank and prestige. Lene has a nobility all her own, and Botho can be as affable and happy among the working people as in his own aristocratic milieu. Once more we ask ourselves why Fontane should insist on erecting the barrier which Botho can so easily forget until the author forces it on his mind again. It may well be that the final dividing line is that between people who have to work for a living and those who don't and who are therefore spoiled for a more frugal and strenuous existence. In every other respect the best of Fontane's aristocrats are truly social and appreciative of the humanity of others, high or low. Botho at the end of the novel somewhat enigmatically maintains that Gideon Franke, the factory foreman who is going to marry Lene, is better than he is. What he can't tell his wife, a slightly silly girl of his own aristocratic breed, is that Gideon will in all probability be a happier man than Botho von Rienäcker.

It is quite possible that Fontane, in spite of all his social philosophizing, was as impatient as his readers must be with aristocratic gentlemen who enjoy the freshness of body and mind of working-class girls but are too timid or too lazy to forgo the advantages of their leisured class. But his style of writing, taken in the widest sense, left him no other choice. Fontane's realism is topographically accurate enough and, as far as events and mores are concerned, so close to his own time that he had to be true to life in all respects. To stage radical opposition to conventions and to arrange for heroic break-outs would have amounted to an idealization incompatible with his diction and composition, to say nothing of his objective observation. Such break-outs occurred only in exceptional cases, to fill the *chronique scandaleuse* of his days. In *Unwiederbringlich* (1891) Fontane treated such a case; the end of the novel is as sad as that of the actual case providing the motif—itself a strong warning against the disregard of the existing order, however provisional this may be.

Irrungen, Wirrungen shows Fontane in complete control of a technique that simulates realism, a chronicling of actual events transformed by imaginative craftsmanship. One of the technical problems—here solved with great skill—arises when after the separation of Lene from Botho the main stem of the story has been split into two parts which, however, are continually kept present in our consciousness, in order to be brought together once again in a meeting between Gideon Franke and Botho. This was a short novel, and the question remained whether Fontane, after his lack of success in *Vor dem Sturm*, would make another more ambitious attempt at narrative structure on the grand scale. He did so and managed well in *Frau Jenny Treibel*, and exceedingly well in *Effi Briest*, while *Der Stechlin*, to be fully appreciated as a narrative, requires to be read in a new perspective.

Effi Briest (1895) takes its place in subject matter beside *Madame Bovary* and *Anna Karenina*. It is the German version of how society deals with adultery, and more particularly Fontane's investigation of society when faced with what is regarded as one of its critical tests, the fall of woman. We may trust Fontane, the ironic respondent to highfalutin words and the tolerant judge of man, to put society and its so-called code of honour in the dock instead of the woman, and to give society a stern lecture, though in the end he may have to acquit the accused, not for lack of evidence with regard to its obsolete standards, but because for the time being there is nothing else to take over its function, which is to provide for rules of conduct and order.

With more than his usual skill Fontane arranges his material in such a way that he does not have to pass moral judgment on any of the characters. Effi, the daughter of a 'Junker' family does not really switch her affections from husband to lover. She accepts the advances of Major von Crampas out of a boredom which, knowing as we do her craving for entertainment, we could have predicted would lead her into temptation. For the Baltic seaport where her

husband occupies a senior government position has little to offer in
the way of distractions. But if the affair is not prompted by love, it
is not a mere flirtation either. Effi invests enough feeling in it to be
disturbed about her transgression, and when her husband is pro-
moted and moves to Berlin she is greatly relieved. There is no repeti-
tion of such a false step, only lingering remorse. Characteristically
this regret is not of the kind demanded by convention. Effi suffers
not because she has committed adultery but because she must hide
the truth; she feels contaminated by a lie. This feeling of impurity
is what causes her sleepless nights; the idea of sin assumes a new
meaning and reacts here on a much more subtle conscience than
society normally prescribes. A finer kind of morality makes its appearance, and though Fontane is not the man to propagate it or fight
for it, its essence is clearly enough suggested by Effi's more delicate
suffering and vulnerability. It is almost seven years afterwards when
her husband, Innstetten, by accident stumbles on a bundle of letters
that bring the past to light. He feels neither disgraced nor compelled
to hate Crampas, but having confided his discovery to his best friend
Wüllersdorf, he is no longer free to act in accordance with his feelings and his reason, even though Wüllersdorf agrees with him and
urges him to let bygones be bygones. The code of aristocratic
tradition asserts itself with a very subtle argument which is as
irrefutable as it sounds far-fetched. Wüllersdorf himself has to bow
to it—now that he has been made to share Innstetten's secret the
latter cannot proceed as if nothing had ever happened. The husband
will have to challenge Crampas to a duel, one or the other of the
two will be killed—the victim happens to be Crampas, who lies in
the sand, mortally wounded and unable to finish a last sentence. Was
he going to say that this was all a very silly affair, thus rising to the
same contempt for a convention which they nevertheless all accept?
Or was he on the point of asking Innstetten to forgive Effi?

The crucial conversation between Innstetten and Wüllersdorf has
been praised as 'die grösste Sprechszene des deutschen Romans'. It
is as dramatic as it is deeply revealing for the mores of the time—
two friends hoping, even pleading, for the same intelligent course
of action and thereby blocking the way for it. But much as we feel
the suspense of a dialogue which only by a hair's breadth misses
averting the death of one person and the divorce and ensuing un-

G

happiness of two others, we realize that Fontane once more regards obedience to the code as the minor evil, a guarantee of some order which is at least better than no order at all. As the chronicler of reality and, in the case of *Effi Briest*, as the author of a succinctly reasoned and superbly composed 'Gesellschaftsroman'—a rare phenomenon in German fiction—he had little opportunity to speak his own mind. That is, not as long as Innstetten and Effi have to be moved on the chess-board of social propriety. Once they are divorced and partly released from social fetters Fontane can develop them into more independent and sensible beings.

Innstetten and Wüllersdorf, when they look back on life, or rather forward to what is left of it, with nothing to imbue them with a strong purpose for living, speak a great deal of the 'Hilfskonstruktionen', the hypotheses that are needed to bear a fundamental resignation with equanimity of mind. Such a feeling of emptiness requires, it would seem, the upper stratum of society as its breeding ground, and it is to the credit of Innstetten and Wüllersdorf, as it is to Effi's before and after her return to her parents, that they conquer a threatening *taedium vitae* by drawing satisfaction from small but indestructible gifts of life, spring returning every year, flowers in the parks, little girls playing with their skipping-ropes, a faithful dog. The intellectuals of a later time proved much more resistant to such simple joys and indulged themselves in a far louder whining about the aimlessness of life.

It is not surprising that the servants of Effi and Innstetten, like all lower-class people in Fontane's works, are in no need of such subterfuges—they have other worries. What is most significant however is that the one representative of the middle classes of whom Fontane gives a full-length picture proves likewise impervious to the malaise of boredom. Alonzo Gieshübler is the apothecary of Kessin, where the Innstettens first live, and a number of characters refer to him as the best person in the town, or even the best man they have ever known. As a hunchback he must have had his bouts with fate, but at the time we are introduced to him he is a master in the art of living, invariably in good humour, always thinking of little attentions to bring joy and amusement. It is not an identifiable belief, metaphysical or religious, that sustains his love of people and fondness for life, so it must be assumed that his adjustment to existence stems from an innately kind disposition and a sense of humour. He is the centre of life in the middle section of the novel, where, even if he has no direct influence on the events, he radiates his *joie de vivre* as a kind of fixed star. If we took our cues from the writers and philosophers of decadence we might conclude that so much *savoir vivre* and refinement of character must have been bought at the price of reduced health and even physical deformity. There is no need to consider such an argument here, and certainly no reason for applying it symbolically to the defects of bourgeois society. We can always count on Gieshüblers to turn up in any period and anywhere, high or low, and in good physical condition at that. All we may concede is that Fontane is aware of the priceless value of men like Gieshübler, or, to come to his last novel, like Dubslav von Stechlin.

Effi Briest is wrought with such technical skill that *Der Stechlin* (1899) comes at first as something of a let-down, a work of failing imagination lacking in cohesive structure and with a plot that serves no other purpose than to keep conversations going. Modern fiction has accustomed us to greater formal flexibility; *Der Stechlin* stays well within the legitimate expansion which the genre can undergo. The *causerie* which looms so large in it comes naturally as an outlet of experience, and as an opportunity to discuss a variety of problems on the level of personal concern and mature insight. The discussion expands with the large number of characters from all walks of life and covers a changing world and its social and political movements. If this makes for so many differences in opinion, it also calls, ideally, for a mind which can discover an underlying order and perhaps arrive at a measure of confidence in life and history.

This is in part achieved through the medium of the central figure of old Dubslav, whose portrait hangs in that gallery which German readers have filled with noteworthy and exemplary literary characters. Truly, he is a man of genuine nobility. But the portrait is also a self-portrait of Theodor Fontane, successively apothecary, war-correspondent, theatre critic, and novelist, an intellectual bred in the middle class of the nineteenth century. The ideal image of man, as bourgeois literature sees it, appears in all manner of human beings. Dubslav has his paladins of equal quality: Barby, the former diplomat, Lorenzen, the Protestant minister serving on Dubslav's estate, the servant Engelke and Mother Buschen, as homespun a piece of living folk-wisdom and folk-medicine as ever shows up in Raabe's works. If they do not all have Dubslav's humour, humility, and irony, his mild-mannered and yet firm exercise of responsibility, and his inveterate fear of fanaticism, they none the less all nestle in the warmth of a really humane atmosphere; they are considerate of their fellow-beings and respect all views honestly arrived at, as if they all remembered Dubslav's saying: 'Etwas ganz Richtiges gibt es nicht.' Those who are not impregnated by this humanity—and there are some—are made to look like ephemeral by-products of true civilization. What impresses the reader most of all is the fact that as if by contact a whole group of people can acquire such humanity and coexist in a spirit of understanding, patience, and serenity. The essence of it all is summed up in the tribute Pastor Lorenzen pays to Dubslav von Stechlin at the funeral. It is not a commissioned performance in idealization, not something that the mourners will dismiss as *nihil nisi bene*. They hear it as a eulogy which they themselves would like to deserve, be buried with and be remembered by. The words were appropriately repeated when Fontane was lowered into the grave: '. . . to speak of his creed, he had not so much the word of it as the deed. He believed in good works and was in the true sense of the word what we ought to call a good Christian. For he had love. Nothing human was alien to him, because he felt himself to be a human being, and as such he was for ever conscious of human weakness. All that which our Lord and Saviour praised and preached and to which he related his promise of bliss—all that was his: a peaceful disposition, compassion and purity of heart. He was what it is best to be, a man and a child.'

This is a towering spire of Fontane's mythology of bourgeois humanism. It takes its place in the skyline of visionary projections side by side with similarly lofty structures springing from socialist or Austrian soil. Peasant literature, for all its down-to-earth ethical purpose, attained on occasion to the same heights.

The last decade of the nineteenth century, as Professor Hatfield points out in his volume, is marked by the stirring of new literary trends, in Germany and elsewhere. Of these, naturalism can be regarded as an intensified realism and a more radical application of its social tenets. But there were other movements, which stood in openly declared opposition to the aesthetic theory and creative practice of the realists. The latter, so it was held, had by and large exhausted the vein of enlightenment and rationality and were coming close to making fiction—and often poetry as well—the handmaiden of historiography, psychology, sociology, and even of journalism. The forces of romanticism, taken in the broad sense of irrationalism and intuition, which had been looked askance at by 'Biedermeier', kept at bay by Young Germany and largely disparaged by the realists, were no longer to be denied and suppressed. The very concept of reality, as it had developed between 1830 and 1890, was ridiculed as a hollow shell sugar-coated with poetic realism, and even condemned as hypocritical and escapist, as a sentimental way of harmonizing the unfathomable and mysterious depths of existence. The social and political engagement of the realists was, if anything, even more suspicious as a concern that is alien to both art and life. Symbolists and cosmogonists, vitalists and solipsists, tried, in their several ways, to expand or change our sensibilities and to shake us out of the ruts of stale custom. They created, if we are to believe their more cautious critics, mainly a spate of private mythologies. But considering the response to Wagner and the influence of Nietzsche and some of his disciples, it must be conceded that the time had come to explore new levels of consciousness and to look at reality from different angles. The literary radicals who were to appear soon after the turn of the century, expressionists, surrealists and others, show by the very strength of their impact an imperative need for bolder modes of existence, or at any rate an awakened curiosity about them. Generations of writers during these turbulent years made it a habit to heap scorn on the bourgeois and to equate him with all that is pedestrian, smug and unimaginative in art and life. This was to be expected. What is astonishing, however, is the fact that while this cauterization of realism was in vogue some of the contemporary writers who commanded the widest interest and received the most assiduous critical attention stood quite obviously in the line of development descending from Immermann, Fontane, Storm, Keller, and Raabe. Much as they varied the technique of realistic narration, as thinkers, mentors and visionaries Thomas Mann, Heinrich Mann, Hesse, Flake, Broch, Musil and Doderer stake their claims in much the same territory in which the realists of the nineteenth century had found such a rich yield in social and political humanism. And it was most likely their interest in the common man—and their desire to communicate with him—that made them also the purveyors of that 'great humour' of their predecessors which in the works of non-realistic modern literature has diminished to a trickle.

Many signs point to a vindication of the nineteenth-century realists. Scholars and publishers have taken cognizance of this by bringing out their works in definitive editions. It is to be hoped that this interest will also be extended to Paul Heyse (1830–1914), and rescue him from the neglect into which he had fallen even while he was still alive. As a friend of many writers to whom he gave unstintingly of his time and experience—being something like the custodian of cultivated diction and especially of the classical form of the novella—he exercised a widely stimulating influence. His large productive output—a number of novels and plays, and more than 120 novellas—is not so much uneven as it is dangerously perfect in style and structure, often so polished as to become impervious to the living impulse of the creative mind. Yet such stories as *L'Arrabiata* (1855), *Das Mädchen von Treppi* (1858) and *Die Stickerin von Treviso* (1871), in which the colourful scene and unbroken vitality of Mediterranean life accord with Heyse's preference for vivid aesthetic presentation, deserve to be remembered; and his novel *Kinder der Welt* (1873) retains its documentary value, informing us, as it does, of an ethically sensitive, cultured but basically insecure German society in the second half of the last century. If nothing else, Heyse provides a measure of the unerring literary instinct which was at work when it relegated him—the first German recipient of the Nobel prize for literature—to a minor but still honourable position in relation to Raabe, Keller, Storm, Fontane and Meyer.

Bibliography

GENERAL ASPECTS

Bramsted, E. Kohn, *Aristocracy and the Middle Classes in Germany. Social Types in German Literature 1830–1900*. 2nd edn., Chicago, 1965

Ernst, Fritz, *Grösse des 19. Jahrhunderts; ein komparatistischer Versuch*. Cologny-Geneva, 1962

Fuerst, Norbert, *The Victorian Age of German Literature. Eight Essays*. University Park and London, 1966

Höllerer, Walter, *Zwischen Klassik und Moderne*. Stuttgart, 1958

Killy, Walther, *Wirklichkeit und Kunstchararakter. Neun Romane des 19. Jahrhunderts*. Munich, 1963

Natan, Alex, ed., *German Men of Letters*, Vol. I, London, 1961. (Essays on Herder, Tieck, Eichendorff, Annette von Droste-Hülshoff, Grillparzer, Hebbel, Storm, Keller, C. F. Meyer, Fontane, Hauptmann, Hofmannsthal.)

Robertson, J. G., *A History of German Literature*. 4th edn., revised by Edna Purdie, London, 1962

Sengle, Friedrich, *Arbeiten zur deutschen Literatur 1750–1850*. Stuttgart, 1965

Staiger, Emil, *Meisterwerke deutscher Sprache im 19. Jahrhundert*. 3rd edn., Zurich, 1957

Steiner, George, *The Death of Tragedy*. London, 1961

Stern, J. P., *Re-interpretations. Seven Studies in Nineteenth Century German Literature*. London, 1964

Sternberger, Dolf, *Panorama oder Ansichten vom 19. Jahrhundert*. Hamburg, 1938

PERIODS; MOVEMENTS

'BIEDERMEIR', YOUNG GERMANY, MARXISM

Bietak, Wilhelm, *Das Lebensgefühl des 'Biedermeier' in der österreichischen Dichtung*. Vienna, 1931

Butler, E. M., *The Saint-Simonian Religion in Germany. A Study of the Young German Movement*. Cambridge (England), 1926

Demetz, Peter, *Marx, Engels und die Dichter. Zur Grundlagenforschung des Marxismus*. Stuttgart, 1959
English Translation: *Marx, Engels and the Poets. Origins of Marxist Literary Criticism*. Chicago, 1967

161

Hermand, Jost, *Die literarische Formenwelt des Biedermeiers*. Giessen, 1958

Hermand, Jost, ed., *Das junge Deutschland. Texte und Dokumente*. Stuttgart, 1966

Hermand, Jost, ed., *Der deutsche Vormärz. Texte und Dokumente*. Stuttgart, 1967

Kluckhohn, Paul, 'Biedermeier als literarische Epochenbezeichnung'. In: *DVjs*, XIII, 1935

Magill, C. P., 'Young Germany. A Revaluation'. In: *German Studies Presented to L. A. Willoughby*. Oxford, 1952

Weydt, Günther, 'Biedermeier und Junges Deutschland'. In: *DVjs*, XXV, 1951

REALISM

Brinkmann, Richard, *Wirklichkeit und Illusion*. Tübingen, 1957

Lukács, Georg, *Essays über den Realismus*. Berlin, 1948

Lukács, Georg, *Deutsche Realisten des neunzehnten Jahrhunderts*. Berlin, 1951

Martini, Fritz, *Forschungsbericht zur deutschen Literatur in der Zeit des Realismus*. Stuttgart, 1962

Martini, Fritz, *Deutsche Literatur im bürgerlichen Realismus 1848–1898*. 2nd edn., Stuttgart, 1964

Preisendanz, Wolfgang, *Humor als dichterische Einbildungskraft. Studien zur Erzählkunst des poetischen Realismus*. Munich, 1963

'Realism: A Symposium'. In: *Monatshefte*, LIX, No. 2, 1967

GENRES

Bennett, E. K., *A History of the German 'Novelle'*. 2nd edn., Cambridge (England), 1961

Closs, August, *The Genius of the German Lyric*. 2nd edn., London, 1962

Dosenheimer, Elise, *Das deutsche soziale Drama von Lessing bis Sternheim*. Constance, 1949

Guthke, Karl S., *Modern Tragicomedy. An Investigation into the Nature of the Genre*. New York, 1966

Kaufmann, F. W., *German Dramatists of the 19th Century*. Los Angeles, 1940

Kunz, Josef, 'Geschichte der deutschen Novelle vom 18. Jahrhundert bis auf die Gegenwart'. In: *Deutsche Philologie im Aufriss*, Vol. II, 2nd edn., Berlin, 1960

Lockemann, Fritz, *Gestalt und Wandlungen der deutschen Novelle. Geschichte einer literarischen Gattung im neunzehnten und zwanzigsten Jahrhundert*. Munich, 1957

Majut, Rudolf, 'Der deutsche Roman vom Biedermeier bis zur Gegenwart'. In: *Deutsche Philologie im Aufriss*, Vol. II, 2nd edn., Berlin, 1960

Pascal, Roy, *The German Novel*, Manchester, 1956
Prawer, S. S., *German Lyric Poetry. A Critical Analysis of Selected Poems from Klopstock to Rilke*. London, 1952
Sengle, Friedrich, *Das deutsche Geschichtsdrama. Geschichte eines literarischen Mythos*. Stuttgart, 1952.
Silz, Walter, *Realism and Reality. Studies in the German Novelle of Poetic Realism*. 3rd edn., Chapel Hill, 1962
Wiese, Benno von, *Die deutsche Novelle von Goethe bis Kafka*. Düsseldorf, 1956
Wiese, Benno von, ed., *Der deutsche Roman*. Düsseldorf, 1963
Wiese, Benno von, ed., *Das deutsche Drama vom Barock bis zur Gegenwart*. 2nd edn., Düsseldorf, 1964
Ziegler, Klaus, 'Das deutsche Drama der Neuzeit'. In: *Deutsche Philologie im Aufriss*, Vol. II, 2nd edn., Berlin, 1960

REGIONS

Bauer, Roger, *La réalité royaume de Dieu. Études sur l'originalité du théâtre viennois dans la première moitié du XIXe siècle*. Munich, 1965
Cordes, Gerhard, 'Niederdeutsche Mundartdichtung'. In: *Deutsche Philologie im Aufriss*, Vol. II, 2nd edn., Berlin, 1960
Eisenreich, Herbert, 'Das schöpferische Misstrauen oder Ist Oesterreichs Literatur eine österreichische Literatur?' In: *Reaktionen. Essays zur Literatur*. Gütersloh, 1964
Ermatinger, Emil, *Dichtung und Geistesleben der deutschen Schweiz*. Munich, 1933
Fehr, Karl, *Der Realismus in der schweizerischen Literatur*. Berne, 1965
Martin, Bernhard, 'Die hochdeutsche Mundartdichtung', In: *Deutsche Philologie im Aufriss*, Vol. II, 2nd edn., Berlin, 1960
Rommel, Otto, *Die Alt-Wiener Volkskomödie*. Vienna, 1952
Schmidt, Adalbert, *Dichtung und Dichter Österreichs im 19. und 20. Jahrhundert*. Salzburg-Stuttgart, 1964

SPECIFIC AUTHORS

ALEXIS

Thomas, Lionel, *Willibald Alexis. A German Writer of the Nineteenth Century*. Oxford, 1964

ANZENGRUBER

Kleinberg, Alfred, *Ludwig Anzengruber. Ein Lebensbild*. Stuttgart-Berlin, 1921

Knight, A. H. J., 'Prolegomena to the Study of Ludwig Anzengruber'. In: *German Studies. Presented to Walter Horace Bruford.* London, 1962

BÜCHNER

Knight, A. H. J., *Georg Büchner.* Oxford, 1951
Martens, Wolfgang, ed., *Georg Büchner.* (Wege der Forschung, LIII). Darmstadt, 1965
Viëtor, Karl, *Georg Büchner: Politik, Dichtung, Wissenschaft.* Berne, 1959

DROSTE-HÜLSHOFF

Henel, Heinrich, 'Annette von Droste-Hülshoff. Erzählstil und Wirklichkeit'. In: *Festschrift für Bernhard Blume. Aufsätze zur deutschen und europäischen Literatur.* Göttingen, 1967
Mare, Margaret Laura, *Annette von Droste-Hülshoff.* Lincoln, Nebraska, 1965

EBNER-ESCHENBACH

O'Connor, E. M., *Marie von Ebner-Eschenbach.* London, 1928

FONTANE

Demetz, Peter, *Formen des Realismus: Theodor Fontane. Kritische Untersuchungen.* Munich, 1964
Remak, Joachim, *The Gentle Critic. Theodor Fontane and German Politics, 1848–1898.* Syracuse, 1964
Reuter, Hans-Heinrich, *Fontane.* Munich, 1968
Sasse, H.-C., *Theodor Fontane. An Introduction to the Novels and Novellen.* Oxford, 1967
Wandrey, Carl, *Theodor Fontane.* Munich, 1919

GOTTHELF

Günther, Werner, *Jeremias Gotthelf. Wesen und Werk.* Berlin, 1954
Günther, Werner, *Neue Gotthelf-Studien.* Berne, 1958
Muschg, Walter, *Gotthelf. Die Geheimnisse des Erzählers.* Munich, 1931; reprinted 1967
Waidson, H. M., *Jeremias Gotthelf.* Oxford, 1933

GRABBE

Bergmann, Alfred, ed., *Grabbe in Berichten seiner Zeitgenossen.* Stuttgart, 1968
Böttger, Fritz, *Grabbe. Glanz und Elend eines Dichters.* Berlin, n.d.

GRILLPARZER

Coenen, Frederic E., *Franz Grillparzer's Portraiture of Men.* Chapel Hill, 1951

Naumann, Walter, *Grillparzer. Das dichterische Werk*. Stuttgart, 1956
Yates, Douglas, *Franz Grillparzer: A Critical Biography*. Oxford, 1946–
(not completed)

HEBBEL

Kreuzer, Helmut, ed., *Hebbel in neuer Sicht*. Stuttgart, 1963
Purdie, Edna, *Friedrich Hebbel. A Study of His Life and Work*. Oxford, 1932
Ziegler, Klaus, *Mensch und Welt in der Tragödie Friedrich Hebbels*. Berlin,
1938; reprinted Darmstadt, 1966

HEBEL

Altwegg, Wilhelm, *Johann Peter Hebel*. Fraucnfeld-Leipzig, 1935
Minder, Robert, 'Johann Peter Hebel und die französiche Heimatliteratur'.
In: *Dichtung in der Gesellschaft. Erfahrungen mit deutscher und französi-
scher Literatur*. Frankfurt, 1966
Zentner, Wilhelm, ed., *Johann Peter Hebel und seine Zeit. Zur 200. Wiederkehr
seines Geburtstages am 10. Mai 1960*. Karlsruhe, 1960

HEINE

Fairley, Barker, *Heinrich Heine*. Oxford, 1954
Hofrichter, Laura, *Heinrich Heine*. Oxford, 1963
Prawer, S. S., *Heine. The Tragic Satirist. A Study of the Later Poetry 1827–56*.
Cambridge (England), 1961

HEYSE

Ferrari, Leonilde, *Paul Heyse und die literarischen Strömungen seiner Zeit*.
Würzburg, 1939

IMMERMANN

Maync, Harry, *Immermann. Der Mann und sein Werk im Rahmen der Zeit-
und Literaturgeschichte*. Munich, 1921
Porterfield, A. W., *Karl Lebrecht Immermann. A Study in Romanticism*. New
York, 1911
Windfuhr, Manfred, *Immermanns erzählendes Werk. Zur Situation des
Romans in der Restaurationszeit*. Giessen, 1957

KELLER

Ackerknecht, Erwin, *Gottfried Keller. Geschichte seines Lebens*. Leipzig,
1939; reprinted Constance, 1961

Lindsay, J. M. *Gottfried Keller. Life and Works*. London, 1968
Lukács, Georg, *Gottfried Keller*, Berlin, 1946
Reichert, Herbert W., *The Basic Concepts in the Philosophy of Gottfried Keller*. Chapel Hill, 1949

LUDWIG

McClain, William H., *Between Real and Ideal. The Course of Otto Ludwig's Development as a Narrative Writer*. Chapel Hill, 1963

MEYER

Henel, Heinrich, *The Poetry of C. F. Meyer*. Madison, 1954
Williams, W. D., *The Stories of C. F. Meyer*. Oxford, 1962

MÖRIKE

Mare, Margaret Laura, *Eduard Mörike; the Man and the Poet*. London, 1957
Storz, Gerhard, *Eduard Mörike*. Stuttgart, 1967
Wiese, Benno von, *Eduard Mörike*. Tübingen, 1950

NESTROY

Forst-Battaglia, Otto, *Nestroy*. Munich, 1962
Weigel, Hans, *Johann Nestroy*. Velber, 1967

RAABE

Fairley, Barker, *Wilhelm Raabe. An Introduction to His Novels*. Oxford, 1961
Pongs, Hermann, *Wilhelm Raabe, Leben und Werk*. Heidelberg, 1958

RAIMUND

Kindermann, Heinz, *Ferdinand Raimund. Lebenswerk und Wirkungsraum eines deutschen Volksdramatikers*. Vienna, 1943

REUTER

Fritz Reuter. Eine Festschrift zum 150. Geburtstag. Ed. Reuter-Komitee der Deutschen Demokratischen Republik. Rostock, 1960

SEALSFIELD

Castle, Eduard, *Der grosse Unbekannte. Das Leben von Charles Sealsfield (Karl Postl)*. Vienna, 1952

STIFTER

Blackall, Eric A., *Adalbert Stifter*. Cambridge (England), 1948
Müller, Joachim, *Adalbert Stifter, Weltbild und Dichtung*. Halle, 1956

Rychner, Max, 'Stifters *Nachsommer*'. In: *Welt im Wort. Literarische Aufsätze*. Zurich, 1949

STORM

Bernd, Clifford A., *Theodor Storm's Craft of Fiction. The Torment of a Narrator*. 2nd edn., Chapel Hill, 1966
McCormick, E. Allen, *Theodor Storm's Novellen. Essays on Literary Technique*. Chapel Hill, 1964
Stuckert, Franz, *Theodor Storm. Seine Welt und sein Werk*. Bremen, 1955
Wooley, E. O., *Studies in Theodor Storm*. Bloomington, 1943

Index